Philly's
Main Line Haunts

Laurie Hull

Schiffer Publishing Ltd

4880 Lower Valley Road, Atglen, Pennsylvania 19310

Other Schiffer Books by Laurie Hull
Brandywine Valley Haunts
ISBN 978-0-7643-3041-4, $12.99

Schiffer Books are available at special discounts for bulk purchases for sales promotions or premiums. Special editions, including personalized covers, corporate imprints, and excerpts can be created in large quantities Tfor special needs. For more information contact the publisher:

Schiffer Publishing Ltd.
4880 Lower Valley Road
Atglen, PA 19310
Phone: (610) 593-1777; Fax: (610) 593-2002
E-mail: Info@schifferbooks.com

For the largest selection of fine reference books on this and related subjects, please visit our web site at **www.schifferbooks.com** We are always looking for people to write books on new and related subjects. If you have an idea for a book please contact us at the above address.

This book may be purchased from the publisher. Include $5.00 for shipping. Please try your bookstore first. You may write for a free catalog.

In Europe, Schiffer books are distributed by
Bushwood Books
6 Marksbury Ave.
Kew Gardens
Surrey TW9 4JF England
Phone: 44 (0) 20 8392-8585; Fax: 44 (0) 20 8392-9876
E-mail: info@bushwoodbooks.co.uk
Website: www.bushwoodbooks.co.uk
Free postage in the U.K., Europe; air mail at cost.

Designed by Stephanie Daugherty
Type set in Marigold/New Baskerville BT

ISBN: ISBN: 978-0-7643-3181-7
Printed in United States

Dedication

To the spirits that walk among us,
may they find peace.

Acknowledgments

L iam Patrick, you are the light of my life. Because of you, most of this manuscript was typed with one hand. Thank you, Jerry Francis of the Lower Merion Historical Society for your time and information. Your stories and your unique way of telling them was an inspiration to me. Rich and Aarika, I couldn't have done this without your help and companionship on my many outings to Lower Merion. Thank you to Lori Clarke for allowing me to use your photos in this book. Finally, a big thank you to my husband Pauric for being so patient while I took ten pictures of the same thing, and Aarika—Why are you taking a picture of trees?

Contents

Introduction

The Beginning of a Community

T he first people to see the advantages of living in the area of Lower Merion area and its environs were the Lenape. They chose the area because of the abundant fish in the river and the plentiful rocks the Lenape call "chert." a stone similar to flint that was used in the manufacture of spear points and arrowheads. The Lenape, like other Native American tribes, had strong faith in, and seemed especially receptive to, the spirit world.

The Lenape believed that there were spirits all around them. They believed that a great spirit created the world and that evil spirits were responsible for sickness and death…Spirits could be helpful or harmful and they had to be treated with respect. "To gain a spirit's favor, people left small offerings in the place where they thought it lived—near a huge tree, a waterfall, or a strange and lonely rock. The gifts might be a handful of leaves or flowers, carved stick, or some pipe smoke. The Indians were careful not to offend the spirits." [1]

These Native Americans were able to live in harmony with nature and the spirits of the Main Line area. They also lived in peace for many years alongside the Swedish, Finnish, Dutch, and Welsh, who were the first European inhabitants of the area we now call Lower Merion. The European settlers didn't need the chert to make arrowheads, but they enjoyed the abundant fish of the rivers and the lumber from the forests. Bringing their own spiritual beliefs, they didn't leave offerings to the nature spirits of the trees of Bowler's Woods, the Hanging Rock, or any other area they inhabited. What happened to those spirits? Were they offended? Is that why this area is so full of spirit activity?

Jerry Francis of the Lower Merion Historical Society related an experience he had in 1997, when three members of the Lenape tribe, who were descended from the original inhabitants, visited Lower Merion. They had traveled here to visit and talk to the spirits of their homeland.

Mr. Francis took them to "Black Rocks" in Gladwyne, which was the site of a Lenape village. He asked them, "Why did they choose this spot for a settlement?" One of the delegation, Linda Poolow, a Grand Chief of the Delaware Nation, answered without hesitation when the spirits spoke to her. She led the group to a large deposit of "chert" at the site even though she had never been to Lower Merion before. She lived in Oklahoma and was not familiar with the sites they would be visiting.

As Mr. Francis and the other men were looking over the "chert," Ms. Poolow began to walk back up to the road. One of the delegates, a shaman from Oklahoma, was selecting a few good pieces of chert when they heard Ms. Poolow calling from the road above. She was standing by the roadside, smiling and pointing at a huge turtle that was crossing the street. The turtle was a major diversion for those people driving down the road. Vehicles were slowing down to gawk at it and swerving to avoid it. Ms. Poolow explained the reason for her joy at this sight. They were being greeted by the giant turtle spirit.

In Lenape mythology, "Kishelemukong, the Creator, brought a giant turtle from the depths of the great ocean. The turtle grew until it became the vast island now known as North America. The first woman and man sprouted from a tree that grew upon the turtle's back. Kishelemukong then created the heaven, the sun, the moon, all animals and plants, and the four directions that governed the seasons."[2] Further, one of the Lenape men present there, who was also a shaman, was from the Turtle Clan!

Is this just a coincidence? Mr. Francis seemed to think it may have been since at the time of the visit the reservoir was being drained. He felt that the draining of the water was what probably what caused the turtle to leave its original home to seek somewhere more hospitable. Some would claim it was pure chance that brought a huge turtle to that spot at the precise hour when it would be most meaningful to those present to witness it. I tend to think that there is something more behind this event.

I have driven down these streets almost every day for the past ten years or so and I have yet to see any turtle, big or small, crossing the road. Does this mean there are no turtles there? Of course not. The turtle shows itself at the right time, when the right people are there to see it. The same can be said for the spirits of this area. They are always there, even if we don't see them. All it takes is the right set of circumstances and the right people for them to reveal themselves.

The Ghost Box

"I shall not commit the fashionable stupidity of regarding everything I cannot explain as a fraud."

~C. G. Jung

A Direct Link to the Other Side

E ver since Thomas Edison made the following statement to reporters, I think people have wondered if it was possible to invent a communication device that would allow us to engage in a two-way conversation with ghosts and spirits.

"If our personality survives, then it is strictly logical or scientific to assume that it retains memory, intellect, other faculties, and knowledge that we acquire on this Earth. Therefore it might be possible to construct an apparatus which will be so delicate, that if there are personalities in another existence or sphere who wish to get in touch with us in this existence or sphere, this apparatus will at least give them a better opportunity to express themselves than the tilting tables and raps and Ouija® boards and mediums and the other crude methods now purported to be the only means of communication."

~Thomas Alva Edison

Although most people believe Edison was joking when he said that, the idea was out there. In 1949, an Italian gentleman named Marcello Bacci Italy starting experimenting with a tube radio to receive the voices of deceased relatives. It worked and people came to Bacci's home to talk with their departed loved ones. This was the first version of the ITC or Instrumental TransCommunication

Device. His work was followed by a Swedish gentleman named Friedrich Jurgenson, who, in 1959, heard what he believed was the voice of his deceased mother during the playback of a recording he had made of birds singing. Dr. Konstantin Raudive, a psychologist from Latvia, was the next big name in spirit voice recording. He started out as a skeptic, but became a believer when he heard the voice of his deceased mother when playing back some tapes he had recorded. Recording of spirit voices is now commonly called "EVP" for Electronic Voice Phenomena, and it specifically refers to voices that are not audible during recording but are apparent on playback.

The ITC idea introduced by Bacci was then expanded on by a man named Frank Sumption, who developed the idea of using randomly generated radio to provide a platform for real-time interactive communication. Whereas EVP was passive, ITC development made spirit voice recording more than just something heard on playback. Frank Sumption also publicized his findings on the Internet, with the illustrations of his schematics for building an ITC device. An ITC device like Frank's Ghost Box gave the researcher an opportunity to converse in a real conversation with the other side. The use of these ITC devices exploded due to paranormal reality shows that featured their use.

When using these devices, it is important to remember that playback is essential. I and others who are experimenting with various versions of this device have noticed that more messages are audible on playback than were noticed during the session. ITC devices range from the original Frank's Box with its detailed configuration to a simple modified radio commonly referred to as the "Radio Shack® Hack." The quality of the sessions seems more dependent on the operator than the equipment, however. I have been able to get amazing results with the "Hack" and I know others have had difficulty getting anything, even with expensive ITC devices.

When you begin a session, it takes a few minutes to start hearing responses to your questions. Once you begin getting responses, it

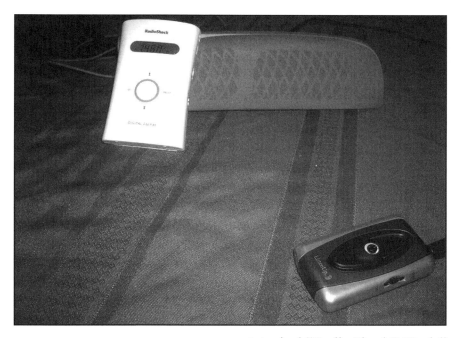

A typical "Radio Shack® Hack."

seems like the radio begins to function in a different way; not as a receiver of radio broadcasts but as a connection, or open channel between this world and the spirit world. It has been my experience that the ghost boxes only seem to work for the person that owns them or the person it was made for. Also, at each session we seem to make contact with the same spirits, no matter where we are. One named Tom has been with us from the first session. These spirits seem to function as controls or guides, and assist in keeping the communication line open. Although it may seem as if you are just hearing random words, the responses are too tailored to the question too often for this to be pure chance.

This is a valuable device in the hands of an experienced investigator, but like any tool used in paranormal investigation, if used improperly or taken lightly, there is the possibility of extremely negative experience and harm to the user. This device should never be used by any person who is not very experienced in psychic self-defense and spirit communication.

Ghostly Goings-On at the General Wayne Inn

Merion, Pennsylvania

The Most Spirited Stop on Montgomery Avenue

I was born in Lower Merion, but I didn't spend much time there after we came home from the hospital. When I did return, it was to this place, the General Wayne Inn, that I was drawn.

I sat in my car in the dark parking area in front of the General Wayne Inn. It wasn't right. There was no way I could go in there. Sadness and loss came off the inn in waves, pushing me back against the seat. "You can do this," I told myself. "It's time to face this thing." I took a deep breath and thought back to another October, about three years prior, when I couldn't wait to get in there.

The Halloween Séance

It was October of 1996 when I got my opportunity to visit the inn. The Barsky show on Y100 was holding their annual séance there. Determined to be a part of it, I sat on the sofa every morning for the week leading up to Halloween—all attention on the radio and my finger on redial. For the first two days I had no luck getting through. Time was running out. It was the day before Halloween and this was my last chance. They asked for listeners to call in who had experiences with ghosts. I couldn't believe my luck when I heard the line being answered, "Y100."

"Hi," I said, hesitating with disbelief, "I have had so many experiences with ghosts it could take up your whole show! I live in a haunted house and whenever I visit a haunted place, things happen. I've been told that I am a natural medium."

"What kind of stuff happens?" he asked.

"Well, doors have opened and closed, pictures have fallen off walls, light bulbs popped, dishes flew across tables. I have experienced all sorts of disembodied knocks, footsteps, etc. Spirits seem to know I can sense them and they like to let me know they're there."

"Can you hold for a minute?" he asked.

"Sure," I answered, afraid to even breathe. I was in! I could feel it.

He came back on, "Can you be at the General Wayne tomorrow at 5 am?" he asked.

"Of course, "I answered.

He took down my name and phone number and hung up. I finally let my breath out.

I was going to the Inn! I ran out to the kitchen to tell my grandmother and ask her to watch the kids.

When I sat down to figure out what I was going to wear, I realized my legs were really cold. "Must be a draft," I thought. My grandmother's house was pretty old and drafty. Strangely, walking around didn't help. As the day passed, I got colder and colder.

By the time I got home that night I was freezing. I piled blankets on me when I got in bed, but it didn't help. Turning up the heat didn't help. Hoping I wasn't coming down with some nasty bug, I tried to get some sleep. Five am was going to be there before I knew it.

I arrived at the Inn a little before five am. I remembered driving by one night with my high school boyfriend, who pointed out the famous haunted place as we drove past it. There was what looked like the statue of a soldier near the front door. It seemed kind of tacky and out of place to me, but

I assumed they were just trying to cash in on the ghostly soldier that was rumored to haunt it. I arrived at the Inn and saw that the statue I saw there ten years ago was gone. As I parked the car, I shivered. The cold from the night before was back even stronger than before.

I walked into an atmosphere of complete chaos. There were people walking around, yelling across the room to each other. Wires and cables crisscrossed the floor and electronic equipment was set up on several tables. If a ghost wanted to talk to me, I hoped I would be able to hear it. A dark-haired gentleman approached me with a big smile on his face.

"Are you here for the show?" he asked.

"Yes," I replied, "I'm one of the psychics."

"Okay, you can come and sit in here with the others." He showed me into a nicely furnished colonial dining room.

"I'm Jim," he said, pulling out a chair from one of the tables and motioning for me to sit, "Can I get you something to drink?"

The dining room of the General Wayne Inn.

I declined his offer and he went over to talk to some of the radio people. I sat there, trying to get a connection to a spirit in the midst of this chaos. I couldn't shake the feeling that there was something to see on the second floor.

We went on a tour of the building, beginning in the bar. I didn't see or feel anything in the bar area. I knew that a Hessian soldier ghost was supposed to be there, but I wasn't getting anything.

When we went to the second floor, I saw the ghost of a young woman crouching in what was then the cloak room. As I was trying to communicate with the extremely traumatized ghost, some of the people in the group were pointing at the chandelier on the landing. It was the strangest thing; Only one crystal was swinging on the whole chandelier! Jim told us that happened frequently and they hadn't been able to figure out what caused that one crystal to swing while the others were still. I turned back to try and help the ghost of the young girl. She looked at me with desperate eyes and her message came through clearly, "There was more than one man, "she repeated as she faded away.

The chandelier with the swinging crystal.

The General Wayne's blinking light fixture.

I shook my head to clear it a little and saw that everyone was still crowded on the landing, looking up at the swaying crystal. Someone shouted from the dining room doorway, capturing our attention. "Look at that! That light bulb is going on and off!" We all walked in to see it.

On the far wall, there were some light fixtures, each with two bulbs shaped like candle flames. One of the light bulbs was slowly turning on and off. The other light bulb in the fixture was not going off.

Ghostly Decorating Advice

We went into the room to get a closer look and Jim began telling us about another odd thing that happened in this room. They had hung a wreath above the fireplace, but they would arrive in the morning to find it *in* the fireplace. The answer to the problem popped into my head immediately. I had an image of a kind of jolly, "hail fellow, well met" kind of man in the room and the idea was coming from him. He thought the wreath was ugly. He wanted a painting put back. It was a painting with horses in it.

When I told this to Jim, he laughed and told me that they had taken down a painting from there to put the wreath up. He wasn't sure if it had horses in it or not, but it was in the attic. Jim called out to the ghost, "We'll try and get that picture back up, okay?"

Meanwhile one of the guys had gone over to get a good look at that light fixture. "The bulb's just loose!" he called out, tightening it. He stepped back as if to admire his effort. "There. That explains that."

I took that opportunity to ask Jim about the soldier statue I saw outside ten years ago. He gave me an odd look. There was no statue here. As far as he knew, there was never a statue at the inn, inside or out.

I then asked him about the female ghost in the cloak room. He nodded as I related what I had seen and heard. "Back in the 1800s a woman was raped and murdered on this landing. You probably saw her. We think that might have something to do with the chandelier."

A couple more things happened that day that didn't make sense to me at the time, but with hindsight were ominous. It started in the dining room next to the bar. There was the ghost of a middle-aged man standing next to the fireplace. He was wearing a hat and a suit and had dark hair and sad eyes. Someone asked me what was wrong and I explained that I saw a man by the fireplace. As I began describing him, people gathered around me. It was clear to me that he was not attached to the Inn, but seemed to be there for Jim, one of the owners. When I related this, Jim, who had joined us, he said that it sounded like his uncle, who had died recently. The ghostly man nodded at that and told me, "I am here for Jim."

Premonitions of Evil

If there was more to the message, I didn't get it because a commotion started at the front of the restaurant. Apparently, Walt Bauer, a man who can see and speak with spirits, refused to enter the restaurant for the broadcast. Barsky was trying to calm an extremely agitated Walt, who was pacing in the parking lot, holding his head and yelling, "Stop it! Stop it! If you don't stop it, I'm going to hurt him!"

I asked, "Whose going to be hurt—Jim?"

The haunted landing – where a woman was murdered long ago.

Barsky turned to me and told us to just go back in because Walt was upset.

"But who is going to be hurt?" I wanted to know, "Is he going to hurt Jim? Maybe we shouldn't have the séance then."

They both just looked at me. I'm not sure why I thought Walt was talking about Jim. Maybe it was because I had just been talking with a spirit who was there for Jim, or maybe it was because I had some precognitive flash of what was to come. I was very uneasy about this whole séance thing now, but everyone else seemed to have a "show must go on" attitude, so I went along.

Then one of the other psychics refused to participate. I could tell something was bothering her, so I asked her what was wrong. "I can't do it," she confided, "I feel like something is trying to take me over—something evil."

I didn't feel like anyone was trying to take me over, but I did feel an underlying current of negative energy through the place. As I tried to determine the source by reaching out with my mind, I could feel that whatever this energy was, it was not human and it was very attached to this piece of property. It was almost as if there was a veneer or wash of *ickiness* over the whole place.

I can't remember who decided where we were to sit during the séance, but there I was, sitting right next to Jim Webb. He was seated to my right and our hands were linked during the séance circle. His hand was ice cold, just like my legs had been. The séance itself was a blur to me. Jim's hand was so cold it felt like I was getting frostbite. This coldness, with the things that Walt said about someone getting hurt, and then the remarks of the other psychic about an evil presence, really bothered me. It was difficult to concentrate on anything else.

After the séance, I couldn't get the Inn out of my mind. Around Thanksgiving I decided to give them a call. I don't remember who I talked to, but I told them that they should leave some kind of recording equipment in the restaurant overnight at Christmastime. I felt they would capture something paranormal that might help us better understand the nature and source of the ghosts of the General Wayne. I often wonder what would have happened if they had taken my suggestion, because on the morning of December 26, 1996, Jim Webb was found murdered in the third-floor office.

I couldn't believe it, but it was true. It was all over the paper and the news for the next few months. After some time, the investigators were finally able to arrest and prosecute the murderer. It was Jim's partner in the restaurant, Guy Sileo. He is currently serving a life sentence.

When I left the inn after the Halloween séance I was convinced there was something not so nice there that was attracting and keeping these spirits. After the murder, I felt that whatever was in there had become stronger, perhaps fed by the tension in the relationship between the owners. It was possible that this energy or entity had influenced the minds of those involved and helped set up the tragedy that had occurred there. With all that in mind, there I was, about to go back in there again because of something else I heard on the radio.

New Owners—Same Ghosts

After it had stood vacant during the fallout from the murder and subsequent investigation, the Inn was taken over by the Abilene restaurant. I was listening to the radio one day near Halloween and heard something that brought a chill to my blood. They were going to have a séance at the General Wayne again.

"Why?" I thought. "Why can't they just let this go? The place has had enough tragedy."

A séance would stir things up again. After a day of deliberating, I decided I had to say something. I wasn't going to just make a phone call that might be ignored. I was going to have to go in there and warn them. They might laugh at me, but at least I could tell them my concerns.

Happily, the person I was directed to was very receptive to what I had to say. She was the promotions director, Carol. She understood when I expressed my reservations about what they had planned for Halloween and she assured me that the séance was really a play being done by actors, so there was no real danger. Motioning for me to follow her upstairs, she then began to tell me about some things they experienced recently at the restaurant. We went up to the third floor and stood in front of a copier, right across from where the murder happened.

She explained that one night as she was leaving, she put a new toner cartridge in the copier outside the third-floor office. When she returned to open in the morning, the cartridge was laying on the floor, opened, toner spilled all over the place as if someone had shook it out.

"You know," she said, "there is no way that cartridge could have fallen out. The copier was open, but I remember twisting it into place and hearing the click. Then I shut the copier. Someone or some*thing* did that!"

I knew what she was talking about. Having worked in three different libraries over the years, I have changed lots of toner cartridges. The cartridges have to be locked in place. Even if they are not properly installed, they still sit down in a spot where they can't just fall out. Still, even if one were to fall out somehow, there is no way that all of the toner would end up scattered across the floor. The cartridge would have to be shaken with force for that to happen.

"The really weird thing is that I asked the cleaning lady if she saw the mess. She didn't even know what I was talking about! She comes in after we close and vacuums and all. There is no way she could have missed it if it was there."

We are left with a few possibilities here. Either the cleaning lady shook out the toner all over the floor and then lied, or someone else did and the cleaning lady didn't see it because she didn't go up to the third floor for some reason. No one ever admitted to dumping out the toner cartridge and Carol said the only person she told about the incident was the cleaning lady and now me.

At this point in the conversation, she had to take a phone call. That was fine with me, because I wanted to absorb everything. When she came back she said, "Okay, Kim, where were we?"

I was speechless and a chill worked its way slowly down my back.

"Kim?" she asked, then hesitated. "Wait a minute, why did I say that? Your name's not Kim."

"That's right," I answered. "It's Laurie."

She began apologizing, obviously perplexed at her mistake. "I am usually so good with names. You have to be in this business. I never do that. I'm really sorry."

Quietly I said to her, "It's all right. I think something wants me to know that it knows me. Kim was my sister's name. She died in a car accident eight years ago. Saying that name is one thing that will definitely get my attention."

"Oh," she answered, "I'm so sorry. Do you want to leave?"

"No way," I replied. I was determined to hear the rest of what she had to say.

Another incident happened to one of the waitresses when she was doing a final walk-through before they closed for the night. As she entered the club room on the second floor—the one with the flickering light—she saw a pillow that had been leaning back on the banquette move forward, tip over and fall onto the seat. It then moved forward and tipped onto the floor. She turned out the lights and went downstairs, shaken. She swore there was no way the pillow could have fallen that way by itself.

Further, she said that the female employees hated going into the bathroom on the second floor. They always felt a feeling of dread as if something bad was going to happen. This is right next to the cloakroom where I saw the female spirit.

We walked down to the cloakroom and looked inside. I didn't see the ghost this time, but we both felt uncomfortable in that area. She pointed to the banquette on the far side of the lounge.

"That's where the pillow lifted up and fell."

As she said this, the light bulb in the fixture on the far wall went out again, then on, then out. It was almost like a Morse code, or someone saying, "Hello." I walked over to the fixture to check the bulb. It was loose, just like when I was here with Y100. I tightened the bulb and walked back towards the hallway.

"There it goes again!" she said and pointed behind me. I turned to see that bulb going on and off again. Taking a deep breath, I went back to the wall and checked it. It was loosened again. I tightened it once more and this time I walked back out. I know that old buildings have tricky wiring that sometimes causes lights to flicker, but tricky light bulbs? Carol walked down behind me, telling me that the light bulb there always flickered.

As we were standing in the hallway, I saw something moving off to my left, towards the stairs to the third floor. I walked over,

Abilene at General Wayne had the same problem.

followed by Carol, and there it was—a woman in a Colonial type dress walking up the stairs. She had dark hair that was covered with a small cap, a light top and a full, dark skirt. I asked Carol if she saw anything. As she answered, "No," the colonial woman put her finger up to her lips as if to say, "Shhhhh." It seemed that this ghost was aware of us and could hear us talking. Although she appeared to motion for us to be quiet, she never actually spoke. As she reached the top steps, she disappeared.

Carol was anxious to hear what I was seeing. When I told her about the Colonial woman she quickly responded, "We had a psychic in here last week and she saw the exact same thing! She said that the lady was telling her to be quiet or she would wake the baby.

This was a ghost that I had not encountered during my last visit. As far as I can tell from the history, it was never a private home. I suppose it is possible that a baby lived there at one time, but it is not likely. During my research on the General Wayne Inn, I discovered another sighting of the Colonial woman. Beth Scott, co-author of *Haunted Heartland, Haunted America,* and *Haunted Heritage* saw the ghost of the colonial woman float right past her as she sat at a table, interviewing Mr. Johnson during her research for the entry on the General Wayne Inn for *Historic Haunted America.* Is this one of the serving girls that appeared during the séance in the 1970s, or is it yet another ghost to add to the list?

About That Soldier Statue...

Before I left Abilene, I asked Carol if she knew anything about the soldier statue. She said she never saw one there and wondered why I asked. I explained that I had the seen one outside the restaurant when I was a teenager. She then asked me if I had gone up to the soldier.

"No," I replied, "Why?"

"Well," she said quietly, "some people have said they see a soldier outside, but it's a ghost. I don't think there ever was a statue. It was a ghost." That was enough to bring that old chill back and keep me looking over my shoulder while I was getting into my car. Is this soldier Wilhelm? Some psychics have reported a Hessian soldier named Max. Perhaps there are two Hessian soldiers there; one outside and one inside.

The Abilene restaurant was at the General Wayne for about a year. About a year later it became a sports bar. That lasted for a couple of years and then it was taken over by the owner of the Seven Stars Inn in Phoenixville, Pennsylvania. That didn't last long, either.

The owners changed, but some things stayed the same. That one crystal would still swing in the chandelier. The basement became so creepy that they had the liquor and other supplies brought upstairs so that no one had to go down there. The third floor in the area of the office continued to be a source of unexplained noises and general unease. Paranormal investigation groups were permitted access to investigate. Although no real evidence emerged, most of the investigators admitted that they felt the place was haunted.

Another View of the Inn

When I visited the Lower Merion Historical Society, they showed me that they have a good view of the General Wayne Inn from their second-floor research room. They also had some interesting information about the ghosts of the inn.

Mr. Francis of the Historical Society said that Bart Johnson, the former owner, was a friend of his and admitted to him one night that he had made it all up! Mr. Johnson thought a ghost would be good for business. He was also something of a practical jokester and had developed a little routine where he would tell stories about the ghostly Hessian soldier to a group of enthralled listeners in the bar while one of his friends would sneak to the basement and wait down there with a broom handle. At the appropriate moment, when Mr. Johnson gave the prearranged signal, his buddy in the basement rapped on the ceiling with the handle, causing the listeners to jump and scream with fright.

In response to his claim that at least one of the ghosts was a fabrication, I told him that I know what I experienced there myself was very real. It was also pointed out that several paranormal groups had investigated and found no evidence of ghosts. These visits or investigations were isolated, one-time things. At the same time, there were persistent accounts from employees and others who were in the building on a daily basis.

One paranormal group said that the flickering light bulb was due to heavy footsteps or dropping something heavy in the room above. That may have happened when they were there, but when I was there, I know there was no one upstairs walking. Anyway, how could walking unscrew a bulb? Even if it could unscrew it once, how could it unscrew it twice?

The Steadfast Soldier

Additional research turned up a report that really throws doubt on Bart Johnson's claim that he made it all up. The first recorded report of a ghost sighting at the Inn was in 1848! This sighting was from when the Inn served as a polling site for Lower Merion Township during the election of 1848. Fresh ballots were stored in the basement of the Inn and one of the volunteers had gone down to get some. She ran right into a Revolutionary War soldier wearing a green coat. This encounter with the soldier's ghost was included in the supervisor's official report to the Board of Elections.

Employees during Mr. Johnson's ownership reported seeing a soldier in green (Hessians wore a green uniform) who would disappear as soon as he was observed. It is unclear whether all of these reports describe the same soldier or several different ones. One employee drew a sketch of the ghostly soldier she had seen in the basement. It was an extremely accurate likeness of a Hessian soldier's uniform, complete with the black hip boots unique to the Hessian uniform.

The presence of a Hessian soldier named Paul was revealed by Walt Bauer, the construction worker turned medium who had a bad premonition at the Y100 séance. In a *Philadelphia Inquirer* article from October 29, 1992, he described the ghost of a Hessian soldier named Paul who complained that there was no "Weiss Bieren" or "wheat beer." Paul described himself as an unwilling soldier who was forcibly taken from his farm in Hesse and forced to fight as a mercenary.

When his regiment was at the General Wayne, one of the barmaids caught his eye and he decided to desert to be with her. He was found out and his commanding officer ordered his execution. The buttons were cut off his uniform and he was buried on the property in an unmarked grave.

Wilhelm was the name of a Hessian soldier spirit who revealed himself at a séance held at the inn in the 1970s. He, like Paul, claimed to have been quartered at the Inn. For some reason, he decided to go for a walk alone at night. Predictably, he was set upon and killed by Patriots. A search party found him the next morning. He was beyond help, but they decided his uniform and boots could be put to good use, so they buried him in his underwear and marched off. Did he walk off into the night in search of good beer? Was he meeting for a secret tryst? Was he deserting? Was he suicidal? It is difficult for me to imagine a reason why a soldier in an invading army would go off alone for a walk in hostile territory at night. In addition, why would the Patriots kill him? He was worth more alive as a prisoner of war who could be traded in a prisoner exchange or even ransomed! Third, if his uniform and boots were so valuable, why would the murdering colonials have left them on him? For these reasons I am inclined to disbelieve this story. Either the spirit was lying to the psychic or the story is an embellished form of another story.

The Secret Tunnel

A more frequently told local legend about the origin of the Hessian ghost is more believable. In this story, whose origins are unknown and attributed to local gossip, the Patriots had built a secret tunnel connecting the cellar of the Inn to another location. Some say it came up in a field, others that it connected to the blacksmith shop across the street. Tunnel or no, it was a strategic location, because it is known that the inn passed from Patriots to British and back on separate occasions.

At the time of the revolution, the Inn was owned by Abraham Streeper, who had purchased it in May of 1776. Streeper was a Patriot who joined the 4th Pennsylvania Regiment. While he was away, his wife ran the tavern. Local hero, "Mad" Anthony Wayne, stayed there on September 13, 1777, while on patrol after the Battle of Brandywine. His troops camped behind the Inn. One interesting account of the inn holds that George Washington and Marquis de Lafayette stayed there as well, but it is unlikely that they did. It is more likely that they stayed elsewhere and just ate breakfast there. The Inn soon fell under control of the British and Hessians after the Battle of Paoli. British General Howe marched his troops into Philadelphia on September 26th. Although they occupied Philadelphia, the countryside around Philadelphia was largely hostile to the British and the Hessians. This was probably due to the British and Hessian soldiers' repeated "foraging" of the countryside in which they seized supplies from the locals. So although the British held Philadelphia, they were not welcome there and were attacked by the patriots in early October in the Battle of Germantown, and later in the winter, the Patriots under, Captain Allan McLane, recaptured the tavern and held it for a brief time before the Hessians regained control.

While the Hessians were celebrating their victory in regaining the tavern, they sent one of their soldiers to the cellar for more wine. He apparently stumbled onto some Patriots who were smuggling supplies from the Inn and they killed him to keep from being discovered. It is said that they secreted his body in the tunnel somehow and that is why he is still there. He didn't receive a proper burial. The only problem with this story is why didn't anyone notice he was missing? Didn't they wonder that he never came back with the wine?

In support of this story, though, is a lot of independent corroboration! The ghost of a Hessian soldier has been seen in the basement by many people, including the election board volunteer. When I visited the in the first time, our tour included the basement. I clearly saw a tunnel of some kind that was no longer there, as well as an impression of people moving things back and forth. Jim Webb told me that there was evidence of a tunnel that had once gone under the road to the shop across the street.

More support for the tunnel story came in 1985, when Mike Benio from Olyphant presented himself to Bart Johnson. He claimed that although he had never visited the Inn he had been compelled to go there to help the spirit of a Hessian soldier named Ludwig. The soldier had been appearing to him every night in his dreams and asked the man to go to the Inn, locate his remains, and rebury him properly. Mr. Benio was a building contractor who claimed that he had some psychic abilities and he believed that the soldier's ghost would guide him to the section of the cellar that needed to be excavated in order to locate his grave.

For some reason, Mr. Johnson allowed this man to dig up part of the basement. Why he permitted this man to do this is unclear if, as he is reported to have said, he "made up the ghost story." During this excavation, an old root cellar was discovered, but there was no evidence of bones or a tunnel. The project was halted when it was discovered that the digging was weakening the structure of the Inn and the parking lot.

The man from Olyphant story is compelling and points towards there being some truth to the body buried in the

Photo of the area that was excavated.

tunnel. How could a person who had never been to the area know which colonial-era inn to approach? A study of inns that existed during the revolution reveals that there were at least twelve in operation in the area. Additionally, the Inn was known as "Streeper's Tavern" at the time of Hessian occupation. Its name wasn't changed to the General Wayne until 1795. So how did he know where to go? It is possible that the man had seen a report on TV or read an account in the paper. The Inn has been featured in Halloween articles and news broadcasts since the early 1970s. *Unsolved Mysteries* had heard of the Inn's haunting and filmed a show around that time. It aired in 1988, and can be viewed on *You Tube* at: http://ie.youtube.com/watch?v=LKQd3UtHpWQ&feature=related.

A Lost Love Token

Another interesting story that appears from time to time in newspaper, book, and Internet accounts of the haunting is eerily similar to the tale that Walt Bauer attributed to Paul. The

An example of an antique photo locket.

story involves a British officer, not a Hessian, who was shot, a locket with a miniature of his sweetheart, and an unmarked grave. During the Revolution, a fatally-wounded soldier was brought into what was then Streeper's Tavern. It is unclear who brought him there or how he was wounded, but he apparently died without telling anyone who he was. He was carrying a locket with a miniature portrait of a young woman.

The soldier was buried in the Stranger's yard of the meeting house next to the Inn. Since no one knew who he was, they kept the locket on display in the Inn, probably hoping that someone would recognize it, or the girl, and put a name to the unknown soldier buried out back. No one ever found out who he was, and the locket remained in the Inn until 1900, when it was acquired by a woman in Merion. I was unable to discover the current owner of the locket, but there are rumors that it is owned by someone in the area. Is this lovelorn soldier one of those that haunts the inn? This story could also be the source of the embellished account about the soldier who took a walk by himself at night, since they were both discovered wounded, carried to the inn, and then buried on the property.

Two British soldiers who were taken prisoner when the wounded officer was brought in were murdered near the Inn and buried nearby, according to some accounts. The prisoners were tied up and held in a stone house across the street from the Inn. When the woman who lived there got home and found the soldiers there, she killed them in retaliation for her husband, who had died fighting the British not long before. The bodies were then dragged outside and buried under the roadway. There they lay, undisturbed until 1830, when digging started for the Columbia Railway. The laborers uncovered bones and pieces of red uniforms. Onlookers took them as souvenirs. In fact, one of the thighbones was found in the attic of a historic home in Narberth in 1885. As if the way they met their end wasn't enough to cause them to want to haunt their murderers, their final resting place was then disturbed and desecrated, their remains scattered all over Lower Merion as macabre conversation pieces! It is believed that these two soldiers also haunt the Inn. If I were them, I would haunt the stone house, but maybe they find the company of all the other soldiers in the Inn more to their liking.

Still Host to Ghosts?

The séance held in the 1970s had reportedly revealed seventeen different spirits. Was there more than one Hessian soldier ghost? Several different Hessian ghosts would certainly account for the variety of stories and names associated with them. The séance psychic made contact with Wilhelm, who stays in the basement most of the time. I am not the only one to have seen a soldier outside, and still others have claimed to see Hessian soldiers in and around the restaurant who have variously identified themselves as Hans, Ludwig, Wilhelm, Max, and Paul.

The General Wayne Inn.

There are clearly two sections of the building.

When I revisited the site in preparation for this book, I made a concentrated effort to try and find the Hessian soldier ghosts. It had been purchased by a Jewish group and was now the Chabad Lubavitch synagogue. I asked the rabbi how they were able to dispel the aura of negativity that had always surrounded the place. All he would tell me is "you dispel darkness with light." I agreed that the building's aura was very light and it was beautifully restored and decorated. The portrait of Anthony Wayne hangs in the reception area in a prominent place. The rabbi showed me an award they had received from the historical society for the restoration they had done. But as most ghost enthusiasts know, restoration stirs things up. It made me wonder about things unsaid. I was curious about their confidence in having dispelled the darkness there.

The Beigenwalds of Woodbury Friends Meeting often told us of little things that happened over the years at their Quaker Meeting House in Woodbury, New Jersey, that let them know it was haunted by a not-so-friendly ghost. The Meeting House had been used as a hospital for some of the wounded Hessians from the Battle of Red Bank. They had cleansed the building a few times, and after a period of relief, the activity would start again. This happens in more cases than people realize. In a place like the General Wayne, I felt that a recurrence of activity was inevitable.

When I visited the Merion Friends Meeting burial ground, I stopped next to the old General Wayne. Immediately, I felt the presence of spirits. I sat for a moment and cleared my mind to try and make contact. I received a clear picture of six Hessian soldiers. They gave me the impression that they had been buried near or under the Inn. My attention was directed to the building, and to something I had never noticed. The "new" part of the building is where the bar used to be. This is the section that was added by Streeper when he purchased it in 1776. I know how long it takes to build an addition now, when all we have to do is run to Home Depot for supplies. It could have taken quite a while back then. It could even have been done in stages. Could there be soldiers buried under that newer part of the Inn? Is that why my attention was directed to the division between the older and newer parts of the building? They had found the two British soldiers nearby when they were digging for the railroad, and no one had even known they were there.

My attention was then caught by the bag that was sitting on the passenger seat of my car. "That's it!" I thought. "The ghost box!" I had been experimenting with it and this seemed like a perfect opportunity, as long as they didn't speak German.

I hooked it up and got started. A voice that identified itself as Paul spoke up right away. I remembered that Walt Bauer had seen a Hessian soldier ghost named Paul by the Inn. "Are you a Hessian soldier?" I then asked.

"Yes. Good."

"Are there Hessian soldiers buried under the new part of the inn?"

"Yes, three."

I also picked up a spirit that said his name was Max, which is another name that has been associated with the Hessian soldier ghosts. I left with the strong impression that the ghosts had left the Inn. They were now hanging around next to and behind the Inn, even more lost than they were before. I told them that they don't have to stay there, that they can move on and be with their loved ones; all they had to do was think of them. I didn't feel as if they did move on, though. I think that, like the ghost at the Woodbury Meeting House, they were just waiting for their chance to get back in.

Sounds like something out of an Edgar Allan Poe story, doesn't it? Cast out spirits, wandering the area, waiting for their chance to regain entry…

Speaking of Poe…

What about Edgar Allan Poe? Wasn't he a guest at the General Wayne Inn? Tradition holds that he was, but I can't see it. First of all, he lived in the city of Philadelphia. Back then, Lower Merion was way outside the city. While he lived in Philadelphia, he and his family lived in seven different houses, none of them even close to Lower Merion. He did travel often between Philadelphia, New York, and Baltimore. None of these travels involve going through Lower Merion. He traveled by train anyway, so he wouldn't have been stopping at the General Wayne. I know that a portrait of Poe once hung in the dining room there and there is a story about him carving his initials on a pane of glass in one of the windows "while he pondered weak and weary" over the perfect words for "The Raven." In reality, he likely "started 'The Raven' at the house on 7th Street in Philadelphia,"1 not at the General Wayne Inn.

Unfortunately, proof of Poe having been a frequent visitor to the inn is lacking. What about that pane of glass with his initials? No photos were ever taken of it and it is said to have been accidentally broken sometime in the 1930s. Besides, it is said that he carved it with a diamond. If Poe ever did own a diamond, chances are he would have sold it. His financial situation, although it was at its best in Philadelphia, was by no means one that would have afforded him diamond jewelry.

What Happened to that Hessian Soldier Painting?

Over the past ten years, I have heard stories about the General Wayne involving a painting of a Hessian soldier. The story claims that the Hessian soldier's eyes follow patrons as they walk through the room. One outlandish version claims that the soldier actually comes to life and steps out of the portrait to confront people who find themselves alone at the Inn late at night. The location of the portrait is described as over the fireplace in the dining room. There were three dining rooms in the General Wayne. The fireplace in the dining room off the bar had a picture above it of the Great Seal of the United States, designed by Lower Merion's own Charles Thomson of Harriton; the eagle with thirteen arrows in one talon and an olive branch in the other. The fireplace in the bar had a portrait of General Wayne above it. This portrait still hangs in approximately the same area today. Now it graces the lounge in the central area of the Chabad Lubavitch.

The main dining room downstairs had a portrait of Benjamin Franklin over the fireplace near the old post office. On the opposite wall was a portrait of Edgar Allan Poe, since he was reputed to have visited there. The upstairs dining room had no portrait above the fireplace. As discussed earlier in this section, the print was of a scene that contained horses.

So what happened to the Hessian soldier painting? Nothing happened to it because there was never a painting of a Hessian soldier there!

Hannah

and the Wayne Family Ghosts

St. David's in Radnor and Waynesborough in Paoli

D oes the soul care about what happens to the body once it has departed it? Logically, once the soul passes to higher realms, it would be unconcerned about what goes on with that decaying flesh buried in the ground. If this is true, then why do we have fears and taboos about disturbing final resting places of people?

So many cultures have traditions and rituals surrounding the death of a person. Traditionally, proper burial rituals are necessary for the deceased, to ensure that their spirit will truly pass on and rest. The issue of proper burial is central in Sophocles' Antigone, so it is clear that our culture has a long tradition of great importance placed on proper burial rites. Perhaps disinterring someone's body undoes the charm that released their soul from their mortal remains and calls it back, bound again to the body they inhabited here.

There are so many cases of hauntings that began with the disruption or desecration of a grave that it is clear there is some connection between them. Many of these hauntings are resolved by re-interment, so I am forced to believe there must be something in the ritual that helps the deceased soul to rest. No wonder, then, that the ghost of General Wayne is said to haunt the area of St. David's Cemetery and Route 322 in search of peace. He should have received a hero's funeral that reflected his contributions to our nation. Instead, his earthly remains were dug up twice, abused, dismembered, and buried in two separate graves hundreds of miles apart.

During the War for American Independence, Anthony Wayne did everything. He recruited, trained, and disciplined troops. He fought in battles and helped to obtain supplies. No assignment was too difficult or dangerous for him to attempt. His nickname, "Mad Anthony" most likely came from the frustrated ravings of a soldier who had been disciplined with a whipping according to Wayne's instructions. The soldier apparently cried out "Anthony is mad, stark mad...Mad Anthony Wayne"[1] over and over again during the beating. The name stuck and he is still known by it today.

Anthony Wayne's military career didn't end after the revolution. Indian tribes, supported by the British, continued to plague settlements on the frontier of the recently formed United States. George Washington called upon General Wayne to lead the campaign in what was then the Northwest Territory. Wayne then recruited, trained, and led a new army to restore order to this area. Within three years, Wayne defeated the Indians at Fallen Timber, and negotiated a treaty that gave the United States all of the land from the Ohio River to the Mississippi. It was his victory here in the Northwest that led to such celebration upon his return home that Streeper's Tavern was from then on known as "General Wayne's Inn."

The General fell seriously ill in Presqu' Isle (now Erie), Pennsylvania, while he was traveling back to Pittsburgh from overseeing the final surrender of the British forts. He died in the Erie Blockhouse. According to the attending physician, he had requested that his burial take place two days after his death and that he be buried in his uniform, in a plain wooden coffin at the foot of the flagstaff of the post's blockhouse.[2] The top of the coffin was marked with his initials, his age and the year of his death in brass tacks.[2] There he rested for twelve years.

I Want My Daddy

For some reason, his daughter then decided that she would rather her father be buried in the family burial plot in St.

David's Episcopal Cemetery in Radnor. General Wayne's son, Isaac, probably figuring that since a dozen years had passed and his father's body was probably just bones by now, set out in a small carriage to fetch the bones. When Isaac arrived in Erie, he asked the doctor who had attended his father's death to deal with the retrieval of the body from the grave. All went well until they opened the casket.

There were no bones. Well, there were bones, but they were still inside a remarkably well-preserved corpse! There was no way that Isaac would be able to fit it into the small carriage. They solved this dilemma in a most revolting way.

Rather than buy a bigger carriage or just forget the whole mess, which is what I would have done, they came up with the idea of boiling the body of General Wayne to reduce it to bones. Since the whole body didn't fit in the cauldron, they dismembered him first. When all was done, the bones were put in a trunk in Isaac's buggy and the water, the General's clothing, and the tools used in this macabre process were reburied in the original grave—minus some locks of hair and one of the General's boots, which were taken by spectators.

With his father's bones in the trunk, Isaac set off for Radnor and when he arrived the bones were buried in the family plot. Legend says that some bones fell out along the way, but contemporary reports indicate that Isaac was very disturbed about the whole situation and regretted that his father's body was treated this way. I feel comfortable in saying that given his documented feelings concerning the treatment of his father's body, it is highly unlikely that he allowed his bones to be thrown out along Route 322.

If Anthony Wayne wasn't mad before, he should be mad now.

Reports persist that the General's ghost wanders the roads between St. David's cemetery and Erie. His spirit appears as a phantom horseman, his head looking from side to side, as if searching the road for something; perhaps the missing bones.

I could find no eyewitness accounts of this phantom, which legend holds rises from his grave every New Year's Day to take to the road again. It's not clear when this phantom was first sighted. Did reports begin after his death? If so, maybe he is still trying to get home. He was called out of retirement to fight the battle of the Fallen Timbers with the Miami Confederacy. He died before he could return to his retirement.

Maybe he can't rest because his grave was not just disturbed, it was violated. There is a replica of the blockhouse where he died in Erie, Pennsylvania. On display there is the original coffin lid, some remnants of his clothing, and the tools used by the doctor to strip the last bits of his flesh from his bones.

"Just a minute," you may wonder, "I thought they reburied the clothes and the tools in the coffin? How did they end up on display?" Well, it seems that the blockhouse burned down in the mid 1800s, and during the cleanup, the exact location of his grave was lost. In the 1870s, there was renewed interest in locating the grave site, and after some research, it was dug up again. It was located fairly quickly and recognized by the distinctive coffin lid and tools. One would think they would rebury these things under a proper monument that couldn't be lost. That's not what they did. For some reason, they decided to display the coffin lid, the tools, and the clothing remnants. The display is still up in the blockhouse today. The grave is empty.

Even creepier is the display that one can see at the Erie County History Center. They have a big kettle, full of water, with some plastic bones floating in it and a fake fire underneath to illustrate the whole ghoulish event. I am surprised he doesn't haunt those places!

Since tradition holds that he rises from the grave in Radnor, I decided to begin my search for the ghost of Anthony Wayne there. His grave was easy to spot; it is tall and has flags and flowers all around it.

As I walked towards the grave, I saw a figure off to my left out of the corner of my eye. When I looked towards it, it was

Monument on General Wayne's grave.

gone. I walked around his grave and the graves of the Wayne family, trying to figure out who was related to whom. I had read an account in a popular book that there was no Hannah Wayne that lived at Waynesborough, so I was surprised to see a gravestone that read, "Hannah Wayne, Wife of William." Her grave was very sunken in, as if something had collapsed underneath. As I took a photo of Hannah Wayne's grave, there it was again—a shadowy figure just inside my peripheral vision that quickly darted away.

Hello, Hannah!

I continued with my efforts to contact the spirit of Anthony Wayne. I stood in front of his grave and said, "Hello! I am here to visit the grave of General Anthony Wayne." I continued to ask questions as I walked around the monument. I asked him if he was at peace, if there was something I could do to help, and if there was something he wanted. All the while, the shadowy figure was jumping in and out of my peripheral vision, almost as if it were playing a game with me. After about an hour of having no luck catching up with the figure or capturing it with my camera, I decided to go back to my car and review the audio recording.

I started the playback and right away there was an unexplained voice! I said, "I am here to visit General Wayne's grave," and a woman's voice chimed in, "Wait." As I backed up the recording to listen again, the shadow was back! This time I saw it clearly in the driver side mirror, walking back and forth behind my car, as if deciding whether to approach or not. I stopped listening to the audio and concentrated on trying to get a clearer view of the shadowy spirit. I did not feel as if this was Anthony Wayne, though, and I know whoever the woman on the recording was, she was also not Anthony Wayne.

I set off to St. David's in search of answers to my questions about General Wayne and I am left with more questions. Who is the shadow? Who is the woman on the recording? And

The grave of Hannah Wayne at St. David's – sadly sunken in.

why does she say, "Wait"? Is it Hannah Wayne, who is buried nearby—the one whose grave is sunken in?

There were rumors of a Hannah Wayne who haunted Waynesborough, the Wayne family home. Did she say "Wait" because she wants to be acknowledged or does she say, "Wait" because Anthony Wayne wasn't able to talk yet? There was no answer on the recording when I asked if he was at peace, but at the end of the session I said, "This is your last chance to tell me what you have to say." This was answered by a very low, whispery female voice. It seemed to say, "I need you …" and the rest was unintelligible. I decided a visit to Waynesborough was in order to see if I could catch up with Hannah there. I was fascinated by the voice on the recording. Maybe she would give me some more details about what she needed at her home.

A Visit to Waynesborough

Which Hannah's Which?

The tour guides at Waynesborough are very knowledgeable and the house has some beautiful examples of period furniture as well as personal documents from the Wayne family. One of the best displays is General Wayne's actual uniform coat. When we entered the front room, I saw a shadowy figure descend the stairs and walk over to my son. I could see a hand reach out as if to touch his cheek. "Baby," she whispered and looked at me. I took a step back, not believing what I was seeing. I asked if anyone was seeing anything, but they shook their heads, so I decided to continue with the tour.

That was a mistake.

The shadowy woman stayed right with us and I had to leave the tour a few minutes later because my son was screaming and would not stay in the house. As soon as we came outside, he was fine, like a switch turned off. When I went back in, he started right up again, so that was it for me. I didn't get to see the upstairs. When my colleagues came out, one of them asked me

Waynesborough – the home of General Anthony Wayne.

if I had seen the little girl run in front of me. "No," I replied, but I told him about the woman I had seen following us.

We decided to ask some of the volunteers about what we experienced there. They didn't know anything about a little girl, but they thought the woman I had seen may have been Hannah, the traditional ghost of Waynesborough. The impression I had was that the woman I saw had been a servant there and I did not feel that she was Hannah. The volunteers at Waynesborough were happy to talk about Hannah of Waynesborough, though. When asked for more information about her and mentioning that I had seen her grave, they informed me that there were no less than three different Hannahs who had lived at Waynesborough.

The first Hannah was Hannah Faulkner, the grandmother of "Mad" Anthony Wayne. She lived there with her husband, who "Mad" Anthony was named after, from the time the old section was built in 1724 until her death in 1763. The second Hannah was General Anthony Wayne's sister, who was born at Waynesborough in about 1747. She married Samuel Van Leer, whose niece was Prissy Moore, infamous owner of the Blue Ball Tavern right up Route 30. Waynesborough was continuously owned by the Wayne family until it was purchased by Mr. Orrin June in 1965. He owned the house until 1980, when it was acquired by the Landmarks Society.

The traditional ghost story at Waynesborough is that Hannah Wayne, who lived there during the Civil War era, was the ghost. "This is it," I thought, "Hannah Wayne was trying to talk to me at the cemetery!" The story I was told by the volunteers was that Hannah was on her way up to the attic one night with a lantern. On her way, she got her nightdress caught in the door and accidentally set herself on fire. She screamed for help, but no one heard her because everyone was outside. In desperation, she threw the lantern at the window. It crashed through the window and caught the attention of those outdoors. Unfortunately, it was too late for Hannah, who burned to death. This would have been Hannah, wife of William Evans Wayne, who lived in the house until she died in 1899. There is no record of how Hannah died, but she did live and die at Waynesborough.

Crash and Burn

Over the years, people have reported hearing the crash of broken glass followed by screaming and crying but no broken glass is ever found. According to the volunteers, the glass breaking, crashing, and screaming is only heard by women. When they began administering the house, Mr. June told them that this phenomenon had been witnessed by an entire dinner party. The large party of several couples was enjoying the main course when suddenly all of the women froze, some with forks halfway to their mouths. They looked around at the others.

The men seemed bewildered. "Didn't you hear that?" all the ladies wanted to know of their partners and host. Not one of the men had heard a sound. The ladies couldn't believe it. They each described hearing a tremendous crash of breaking glass from upstairs. Mr. June promptly investigated, but could find no broken glass.

In a similar incident, one of the caretakers reported that, one night, all her china was thrown out of a wall cabinet and landed on the floor in a tremendous crash. All of her dishes and dinnerware was smashed. The current caretakers have reported no such incident, and the volunteers I spoke to, who were ladies, said they have never heard the crash, but they have seen the woman in the fireplace.

There was a woman in the fireplace? I was intrigued. The guide took me right upstairs to point it out. There, in the best bedchamber, on the back wall of the fireplace is the clear image of a woman. The image is burned into the wall and is extremely clear. Photographs are not allowed in Waynesborough, so you will have to go visit and see it for yourself! Considering the legend of Hannah burning to death, it seemed like an incredible coincidence. Hannah was obviously trying to communicate for some reason. Maybe she wanted to tell the truth about how she died. Maybe she was just upset about the condition of her grave. I was determined to find out, so I set off for a return visit to the cemetery. This time I brought one of my group members with me.

A Heart to Heart With Hannah

We walked up to the grave of Hannah Wayne and saw that it was even more collapsed than it had been. We asked Hannah if she burned to death. The answer we got on the recording was, "What?" I repeated the question, but there was no response, so we were still unable to get any clues as to how she died. The next question was, "Hannah, do you want to talk?" The response on the audio recording was very clear. The voice of

**Another view of Waynesborough –
Is one of these windows the one Hannah smashed?**

a woman says, "You want to help me out?" I continued with the questions, asking her what she wanted, if she needed anything, and if she was concerned about the state of her grave. There were no further answers from Hannah. I asked about the woman I saw at Waynesborough. We looked around for a groundskeeper to ask them to fix the grave, but there was no one there that day.

We walked around the Wayne family plot, trying to figure out the relationships. When I got to one marker, I had to call my colleague over. It was the grave of a five-year-old-girl. The inscription read, "Sidney Wayne, daughter of Isaac and Elizabeth Wayne." According to this marker, she died in 1817, when she was five years old.

The records at Waynesborough contain nothing about a child who died there, nor do they contain records about servants. If only those walls could talk!

Grave of Sidney Wayne – Is she the little girl at Waynesborough?

Waynesborough is located at 2049 Waynesborough Road in Paoli, Pennsylvania. They are open for tours Wednesday to Saturday, from 1-4 pm from April till December. For more information, visit their website at: http://www.easttown.org/GeneralInformation/history/waynesborough.htm

"An idea, like a ghost, must be spoken to a little before it will explain itself."
~Charles Dickens

What about that Shadow?

I am still not sure who or what the shadow was. When I returned to Waynesborough with my associate to do some investigating, he noticed the tops of crypts right behind where we parked. That was the area where I'd seen the shadow pacing the last time I was there. We found a path and it led to a grassy area with a creek on the right and a row of family crypts on the left. As we walked down the row of the crypts, we noticed that there were a large number of crows in the area. Then we saw that the last three were open and empty, except for the crows flying around them. In front of the crypts were large storage containers.

We surmised that they were repairing the crypts and had moved the occupants into the storage containers. There were two crypts that gave me a feeling of being watched. One of them was open and one was still locked. I approached the one that was still locked and seemingly occupied.

I had my recorder in my hand, but hadn't turned my camera on yet when— *Whoosh!*—something black flew right in front of my face, causing me to stumble backward and lose my footing, nearly tripping over a stone bench that was hidden under the ivy that nearly obscured the sides of the crypt. My first thought was that it was a crow, but I realized very quickly

The crypts and the containers.

The Wilbur Mausoleum – Where I encountered a black shadow.

that it was not a crow. It had been way too large to be a crow—and it was silent. If it had been a crow, I would have heard some kind of flapping of wings at least.

Although I was a little shaken, I decided to try and see if the spirit would speak to me on my recorder. I asked if there was anyone there and what they wanted to say to us. Upon playback the answer to my question about what they wanted to say to us was a very rude expression and the first negative EVP I have obtained in ten years of EVP research! Was this the shadow from the first day I was there? If so, who was it and what did it want? Subsequent visits have not provided any answers, so the mystery of the shadow remains unsolved.

A Bloody Vision
at Paoli Battlefield

Malvern, Pennsylvania

My first thought was, "How the heck did the British ever find this? I have lived in this area most of my life and I couldn't find the place!" It didn't even look like a typical battlefield park. It was more like an extension of someone's back garden. There were lots of trees, benches, and people walking dogs. On the surface, it all looked so peaceful. As we pulled up to the battlefield, I saw that there was a large stone square fence area with a monument in the center, and it was here I was drawn to first.

Monument over the graves of the fallen soldiers.

As I walked towards the area from the car, I felt the first of the cold spots. It was just a brief chill, but it was enough to let me know there was someone here saying hello. Was it a fallen soldier? I had to wait and see. When I reached the monument, I saw that the stone fence enclosed the burial place of the fallen Patriots of the Paoli Massacre.

I walked around to the front of the monument and the feeling of a presence grew stronger, pulling me to the far side of the squared-off area. Immediately, I was hit with the message that I should be looking at the ground, looking for something. There was a lot of quartz-type rocks on the ground, but not much else, so I continued on to the far side.

As I stepped past the wall, my chest instantly tightened and it was difficult to breathe. My mind was full of images of a horrific murder scene. I saw a young man who appeared to be a soldier. A larger soldier in a dark coat was stabbing him in the stomach with what seemed to be a long stick. As he stabbed him, I felt the sensation of blood filling my mouth as I struggled to get my breath following the attack. He fell to the ground, and I was still feeling every gasp as the attacker placed his foot on the fallen soldier and yanked the long stick out of his body. The fallen soldier rolled to his side and his eyes pled with me, sending me a silent message, "Please find it. Please." I wished it were that simple. I had no idea what *it* was he wanted me to find, but I know that he felt it was still there.

At the same time, the colleague I had brought with me that day walked up to me and said, "Ooh, wow! I really feel something over here. I feel like I just stepped into an electrical field or something." I nodded, afraid to speak. I didn't want to tell him what I had seen because I wanted to see if he would pick up anything about it.

The vision was over, but it left me a little shaken and confused. Why would the spirit show me this scene, but not the thing he wants me to find? I could still feel him there, off to my left, waiting and watching. We decided to do some recording to capture an EVP. Maybe he would tell us on tape what he wanted us to find.

At one point on the taping, I asked "Were you British or were you a Patriot?" My companion and I both shivered and looked at each other. The air had suddenly grown thick and the message we got was clear to both of us. "How can you not know?" We looked at each other and said, "Patriot," at the same time.

After the taping, I tried again to concentrate on the young soldier. I sensed that his name was Samuel. He was telling me that he tried his best. He kept repeating this and I tried to assure him that we all know that they did their best, and their efforts were not unrewarded, as our nation gained and kept its freedom from Great Britain.

As we walked back around, we saw a small group of older people at the entrance to the field. We greeted them and told them that amazingly, although we have lived in this area most of our lives, we have never been here. They nodded in understanding. They hadn't been here in about ten years themselves. The man told us that ten years ago the park looked completely different, all run down and overgrown. He said it has only been in the past few years that they have taken an interest in maintaining and cleaning it up. He also told us that this battlefield is one of the only ones that still look almost exactly like what it did the day the battle happened. Maybe that's why the memories of the battle are still so close to the surface.

Shadow Soldiers

We decided to go back down the path into the woods, past the area where we had felt the spirit of Samuel. I sent my friend on ahead and decided to go back to the car and review the tape. As I sat listening, I noticed the people we had been talking to were leaving. As they got in their car I glanced back towards the battlefield. A shadowy form of a man was standing there at the gravesite, facing me.

As I watched, the shadowy man began moving towards me. As he reached a large tree he disappeared. Was it Samuel? I don't know. I decided to get out of the car and take photos. Nothing anomalous showed up in the photos I took, but there was a feeling of anticipation that was difficult to define, it is almost like when you know something is about to happen, like when you are playing *hide and seek* and you know someone is going to jump out any second and yell, "Got you!" I also picked up an image of men dragging other men and large sacks back across the roadway.

I saw my buddy returning from his trek down the path. He walked up and said, "You know, I have a feeling like someone was bayoneted in the stomach." My companion that day was Rich, a veteran Civil War re-enactor. I loved bringing him to battlefield sites because he can explain some of the messages and images that I get from the ghosts of soldiers. "Okay," I said, "I had the same thing over there by the bush when we were recording for EVPs."

Path where we encountered the ghostly vision of a soldier.

When we returned to the spot, the same feeling was still there—minus the bloody vision, thankfully. We both went down the path, and I stopped at a couple of spots where I felt something might be there. The main feeling I had in the woods was a sensation of someone running away and feelings of confusion and panic. I also had a vision of smoke, so thick it obscured vision and made it hard to breathe. I could feel men running, without direction, in the dark. I was told that there were soldiers in green who were not Patriots. They seemed to be British soldiers, not Hessians, which was confusing to the spirit. I asked Rich if there were Hessians at this battle. He said there weren't, but there was a unit of British soldiers at this battle whose uniforms were green.

A Brutal Attack

It was time to walk around and find out more about the battle and see if our impressions matched what happened there. General Wayne had been sent to this area after the Battle of Brandywine to try and slow down the British advance to Philadelphia. The troops were camped in tents all along the tree line at the edge of a field. In the early morning hours of September 20th, the British troops, led by a Lord Grey, crept up on the camp. They had been informed of the camp site by spies loyal to the Crown. Grey ordered his men to remove the flints from their rifles so they didn't accidentally discharge, and they arrested all the civilians on their way so that the Patriots wouldn't be forewarned. General Wayne was warned of the attack by a farmer whom he met when he stopped in the Paoli Inn that night. It is not known what Wayne's plan was, but he was not taken completely by surprise as some have said. Still, the severity and manner of attack was unexpected and over 100 Patriots were killed or wounded before an effective defense could be mounted to cover the retreating Patriots.

This attack by the British was thought of as especially brutal because they snuck up on the camp at night and used bayonets to attack. Additionally, when the British attacked that night, the captured and wounded Patriots were then killed or injured. In all, there were about 50 Patriots killed and about 200 injured out of 2200 troops when the battle was over. This is why it was called the "Paoli Massacre," and the British soldiers feared retaliation for this attack throughout the remainder of the war.

This battle haunted General Wayne as well and many accounts of his life hold that he believed it was the low point of his military career. There were accusations of misconduct on his part, and to put these charges to rest, Wayne demanded a court martial of himself. He was acquitted of the charges, but as the commander, he probably felt responsible anyway.

Was there a soldier named Samuel that died at the Paoli massacre? After some research, I found a listing of some of the fallen at http://www.ushistory.org/Paoli/history/casulatiesalph. htm. On that list there are two Samuels who were wounded, two that were MIA, and one who was captured. While it's possible that the Samuel that was captured later died, and that it is his spirit that returned to the battlefield where he believed he lost something, there is no way to know for sure.

This battlefield, like most, has an overshadowing feeling of sadness and loss. Is it haunted? Yes, it is haunted by at least one ghost that we encountered, and I strongly feel there were more ghosts there waiting to show themselves to the right people at the right time.

The Headless Horseman of Paoli

Move over, Sleepy Hollow. We have our own headless horseman ghost right here. He's the ghost of a Revolutionary War soldier from the Battle of Paoli. He gallops down the roads near the battlefield. If you see him, you're doomed to die within the year. I first read this story in another ghost book, but could not find another account to lend it credibility. But since the author wasn't at the battle, the story must have come from somewhere. I finally hit the jackpot with a lucky combination of words in a search on Amazon.com and found a story in an out-of-print book called, "The Headless Horseman of Paoli." It was a very fanciful, obviously fictional, account of the story I had read. After checking the bibliography, the truth was clear. "The Headless Horseman of Paoli" was originally published in the October 1980 issue of Fantastic Stories. Fantastic! It was a great story, but not a true one.

Haunted Harriton House

Bryn Mawr, Pennsylvania

"Where'er we tread 'tis haunted, holy ground."

~Lord Byron

Haunted By a Folktale and a Founding Father

My first thought on viewing Harriton House was, "Wow! What a gorgeous house!" Luckily, the day I chose to visit was a slow one and I had Harriton and the guide all to myself.

The inside is as beautifully and immaculately kept as the outside. Although the guides are friendly and extremely knowledgeable about the history of the house, beware of asking about the ghosts associated with Harriton, especially that of "Tuggie the Witch." It is not advised. The guides' distaste for the mention of ghosts is understandable. Association with a legend like that of "Tuggie" rather than the founding father and the real ghosts of Harriton would be annoying. I considered not even mentioning the legend of Tuggie, but then thought perhaps I should begin by putting this distasteful legend to rest.

The Legend of Tuggie

The story of Tuggie began during the time of Richard Harrison's ownership. He was a wealthy Quaker who had relocated to Pennsylvania from Maryland, bringing his slaves with him to run his tobacco plantation. Tuggie is said to be

Harriton Plantation – Home of Charles Thomson.

one of the slaves who had great magical powers. Some versions of the story hold that Tuggie was angry at being brought to Harriton, and others swear that she was angry because she was going to be sold. In either case, the actions that Tuggie is said to have taken to remedy her situation seem pointless in accomplishing either goal of being reunited with her family or taking revenge on her owner. To get revenge on Harrison, she went to the family burial yard at night to drive a stake through the heart of his recently deceased daughter. For some reason, before she left, she also left a poisoned cup of chocolate for Harrison to drink. Overkill? Perhaps. A bit of added drama? Likely. It seems completely illogical to poison someone and then set out to abuse a corpse in order to avenge oneself. It would be very difficult to get revenge on a person who was already dead from poison.

Now Tuggie was not one to be deterred by things like logic. She is said to have gone to the cemetery at midnight and driven the stake into the grave, deep enough to pierce the heart of the corpse. Again, I am left wondering how this is possible, and even if it were, how would one know whether or not the heart of the corpse was pierced?

Fortunately for Mr. Harrison, Tuggie pierced the hem of her skirt rather than the heart of the deceased and promptly died from fright when she could not run from the grave. At the same time, Mr. Harrison heard her scream of fright and jumped, spilling his poisoned chocolate on the floor. It was lapped up by the family cat that died instantly. Poor Tuggie's ghost is now said to wander the property in a perpetual state of terror. Indeed.

I can assure you that Tuggie, if she even existed, did none of the things she is accused of and does not haunt Harriton. This story is a folktale. In my research on haunted places around the world, I have found various version of the same legend. The most common version is that of people who dare one of their friends to drive a stake, stick, or knife into the grave to prove their bravery or to win a bet. The person does so and their coat or hem is accidentally caught with the stake, causing them to either die or pass out from fright. Sometimes they wake up on the grave and all of their hair has turned white overnight.

The Apron and the Grave

One example is this account from *Hoosier Folk Legends* by Ronald L. Baker.

"In the early part of the 1880s, some teenaged girls visited a farm to attend a corn shelling party. When it became dark, they began telling stories concerning the cemetery. Soon they were daring each other to enter the cemetery. One girl declared that she would not only enter but would plunge a knife into a grave. When she did not return in a reasonable time, the adults searched for her. They found her dead, slumped over a grave. She had placed the knife in a grave, but is so doing had anchored her apron to it and died of fright."

This classic legend is also known as "The Graveyard Wager" and has many variations. One version can be found at http://urbanlegendsonline.com/classics/gravewager.html. Written versions that are nearly identical can be found in *A Night with the Hants & Other Alabama Folk Experiences* by Ray B. Browne and in *Buying the Wind: Regional Folklore in the United States* by Richard M. Dorson. Harriton's "Tuggie the Witch" is our local version of a popular folktale. The folktale is always adapted to include local references that make it seem more real.

Obviously, this legend of "The Graveyard Wager" illustrates our fear of death and hints at how irrational it is, since it is not a ghost or revenant that kills the victim, but her own fear. This lesson can be applied to the paranormal as well. The biggest obstacle for many people in being open to experiencing the paranormal is overcoming their fear of it.

A Forgotten Founding Father

The real story of Harriton is less dramatic than the folktale, but no less interesting. Richard Harrison's daughter, Hannah, inherited Harriton and married Charles Thomson when she was forty-four years old. He had arrived in America a penniless Irish orphan in 1740, and thirty-four years later he married Hannah Harrison, who was a wealthy heiress. He also became one of our least-celebrated founding fathers. He was the first and only secretary to the Continental Congresses. He was so closely ranked to President George Washington that Thomson stands to the right of John Hancock in the painting of the Declaration of Independence seen on the two-dollar bill. Another little known fact is that John Hancock's and Charles Thomson's are the only two names on the Dunlap broadside, the original copy of the Declaration printed the night of July

4th—another copy was made later, which is the one familiar to most of us. His most lasting accomplishment is that Thomson designed the Great Seal of the United States. The United States of America continues to use the Great Seal on all of its official documents. It is also found on the reverse side of the one dollar bill.

Charles Thomson traveled to Mt. Vernon in April, 1789, to inform George Washington that Washington had just been elected first President of the United States under the new Constitution. Although some historians site this as further evidence of his close relationship with Washington, this was actually a political intrigue planned by some of his rivals. While he was away, they voted him out and had him removed from his position as secretary, saying that the position was no longer necessary.

Fed up with politics, he retired to Harriton House. He and his wife never had any children and they never owned any slaves. When Hannah inherited the slaves with the plantation, she educated and freed them. They were seemingly happy at Harriton, entertaining guests like the Kerwins, whose portraits grace the living room walls, and Thomas Jefferson, who was known to take tea with them. Charles had time now to develop some of his progressive agricultural ideas and write an English translation of the Bible. So why does his ghost still walk the grounds of Harriton?

A Penetrating Gaze

A neighbor of Harriton House was returning home around 3 am one morning. As he entered the circle by Harriton, he noticed two figures walking on the lawn of the old house. One of the figures was tall and one was short. The shorter man was wearing a hat like those that a farmer would wear. At this point it struck him that the figures were very clear to him in spite of the fact that it was pitch dark. The figures themselves seemed to be lit somehow, so he was able to watch them as he neared the end of the circle.

The Portrait of Charles Thomson.

As he parked the car, he looked in the rearview mirror and was struck by the image of the taller man's eyes. He said he could only describe them as stern and hawkish. The image of the tall man's eyes was imprinted in his memory to the degree that when he then attended an open house event at Harriton, he instantly recognized the eyes in one of the portraits hanging in the historic home. He asked one of the guides who it was and they responded with pride, "Oh, that's Charles Thomson. He was the most famous resident of Harriton."

During my visit to Harriton, I viewed his portrait, and I must say that he does have a rather penetrating gaze. I did not see the spirit of Mr. Thomson, but I did feel that he was not at rest. My feeling was that his unrest was tied to his final resting place being disturbed. I asked the guide about the family cemetery, located nearby on private property. "Is it possible that his spirit is not at rest because his grave was disturbed?"

Lurking in the Living Room

At this point, I heard a rustling noise from the living room. I walked over and looked in. There was nothing there. I glanced up at the portrait of Charles Thomson, "Do you think Mr. Thomson was happy with his life?" I asked the guide. I was

Harriton's Parlor – Where someone was rustling papers.

getting a strong impression that Charles Thomson felt cheated somehow—like he deserved so much more recognition than he got.

"Probably not," she said, "He was very bitter over the secretary position being eliminated. I believe he felt that he deserved more recognition or credit for his accomplishments."

There was more rustling from the living room. Again, when I looked in, there was nothing that I could see as the cause of the noise. It sounded just like someone shaking a bunch of papers. It was similar to the sound caused by turning the pages of the newspaper.

A Grave Problem

Trying to get to the bottom of things, I asked her, "Was his grave really dug up? That has been known to cause a person's spirit to haunt a place."

She answered, "We're not sure whether he was actually dug up. Some of the graves were dug up, though."

The graves were dug up to help sell burial plots at the "new" Laurel Hill Cemetery. One of Charles Thomson's relatives was asked if the Thomson's could be re-interred there. It seems that people would be more likely to buy plots in a cemetery if they could spend eternity next to some local notables. Representatives from the cemetery approached the relatives of notables like the Thomsons and offered them payment for allowing their famous relatives to be reburied at Laurel Hill.

The only problem was, there were no markers for Charles and his wife in the family plot. So they dug up the graves that they believe were those of the Thomsons. Charles Thomson died in 1824, and Laurel Hill was started in 1836. By that time, there were nineteen people buried in the family plot. Locations of individual graves was from memory. They probably got the right graves, but it's possible that they didn't.

"That's enough to make my blood run cold," I thought to myself. "If one of my relatives did that, I'd probably haunt them, too."

I went back for one last look at the living room. A chill passed through me and I had the strong feeling that someone was watching and listening. I assured the guide and the present spirits that I would make sure that Charles got the recognition he deserved. So if you find yourself near Harriton House, stop by for a visit. Let Charles know you stopped by to see the home of the famous founding father. Maybe when he gets the recognition he deserves, his spirit will rest at last.

Harriton is located at 500 Harriton Road in Bryn Mawr, Pennsylvania. There is usually someone there, but it is best to call if you want a tour. Their number is: 610-525-0201. You can find more information about Harriton House at their Web site, http://www.harritonhouse.org.

The Sad Spirit
of John Roberts House

Bryn Mawr, Pennsylvania

John Roberts III was a successful man who, in 1774, owned 420 acres of land, a grist and saw mill, and a paper mill, in addition to being partner in other area mills. He also owned and lived in a large stone dwelling at the corner of Old Gulph Road and, what is now, Mill Creek Road with his wife, Jane, and ten children, as well as many servants. He is the one who expanded the original house, built in 1690, by adding a 3.5 story addition. The Roberts family were Quakers and as such, pacifists. This did not sit well with some of his Patriot neighbors. If someone needed help, John gave it to them. According to Mr. Francis at the Lower Merion Historical Society, the trouble really started when some British soldiers were walking along the road and asked John for a lift. He had room, so he agreed. They were seen conversing and smiling, with Roberts apparently pointing out some of the local points of interest along the way. Unfortunately for Roberts, the British launched foraging raids based on the information they got from Roberts. Foraging raids were little expeditions that were done by both sides. During one of these raids, the soldiers would seize livestock and provisions to supply the armed forces.

Gossip spread about Roberts and was embellished to include the accusation that he had mixed ground glass into the flour that he sold to the Patriot troops. On the night of October 10, 1777, things reached the boiling point and a mob was formed to confront Roberts. Some accounts hold that the really vicious gossip and incitement to attack all came from one of Roberts' neighbors who had designs on his property. After receiving several threats and accusations of being a Tory, Roberts decided to relocate to Philadelphia until things settled down.

The unruly group of vigilantes came to the miller's house and demanded his surrender. They planned to hand him over on the spot for treason. His sons refused to open the door. The mob was so full of blood lust that they hanged Roberts' hired man, Mr. Fishburn, and also stole sixty-four animals. Incensed, Roberts wanted to return home immediately, but his sons begged him not to because they feared for his life.

True to his good character, Roberts tried to help Patriots who were imprisoned in British-held Philadelphia. He tried to help by petitioning people of influence, detailing abusive treatment

Does John Roberts still haunt his home on Mill Creek Road?

the prisoners received by the British soldiers. "At some point he was forced to guide British soldiers on foraging raids in Lower Merion...his only assistance to the British."1 If he were really a British sympathizer, he would have left with them when they left Philadelphia in the late spring of 1778. Instead, he turned himself over to the Patriots and swore an oath of loyalty to their cause. He also gave them information he had gathered on the British plans for future troop movements and campaigns.

Apparently, this was not enough for his neighbors because they submitted sworn statements against Roberts and he was arrested around the end of July for high treason. He was quickly tried and sentenced to be executed. Petitions to spare his life were begun by friends and supporters. Among these supporters were three signers of the Declaration of Independence. In spite of that, he was hanged on November 4, 1778. All of his property was confiscated. His wife was allowed to retain only those things that she could prove were part of her dowry.

By the latter part of the 1800s, the once-impressive house was abandoned and was falling into ruin. Some people believe that it was during this time that it gained a haunted reputation. It's not clear what started the rumors of a haunting there, but enough unexplained events have happened since the house was rehabilitated and reoccupied that the house really does host at least one resident ghost.

The first account I could find concerning the ghostly presence there was the report in a *Main Line Times* article in which a teenaged couple was sitting on the living room sofa. They heard footsteps by the front door, which went right up the stairs. They described the footsteps as sounding like heavy boots. Upon investigation, they found that they were alone in the house. This was sometime in the 1940s.

The next account came from two women who lived in the house sometime before the current owners. The women described seeing a silhouette of a person standing at the window. The silhouette was of a slim person with a ponytail,

wearing what looked like a dress. The current owner believes they may have seen a Colonial-era man, who would likely have had a ponytail and worn a frock coat that could easily be mistaken for a dress when seen in silhouette.

Workmen who come to do repairs have reported feeling a presence and residents have heard their names called when they are in the house alone—all typical markers of a ghostly presence. Some believe the ghost is that of John Roberts, whose neutral stance in the War for Independence cost him his life. Others think a likely candidate is poor Mr. Fishburn, who was murdered by a bloodthirsty lynch mob because he happened to work there. I think that the current atmosphere of the house is so welcoming that they may both be there. The house, a mansion by Colonial standards, is certainly roomy enough for both of them!

All that remains of John Roberts' Mill on Mill Creek Road.

The Blue Ball Inn's

Murderous Mistress

When Mr. & Mrs. Kehler decided to purchase the house that was once the infamous Blue Ball Tavern, they knew they were getting a piece of history. I don't know if they really believed they were getting a ghost, too. When they went to look at the house, the former owner told them that the infamous Prissy, who once ruled the Blue Ball with an iron fist, was buried right up the road. They hopped into the car to go see her grave at Great Valley Presbyterian Church. They started in the old section, trying to decipher the old names on eroded headstones.

"You go that way and I'll start looking here," said Mr. Kehler to his wife.

**The old Blue Ball Inn –
Showing the original and the newer sections.**

He began reading the names on the graves, but he hadn't gotten very far when his wife called out, "I found it!"

"It was like she led us right to her grave," he told me, "Of course, we bought the house."

It's hard to believe that this beautiful, old historic home was once a low-class rough-and-tumble tap house that catered to the lower classes—pack peddlers, itinerant merchants, immigrants, and the like. The female owner of this shady establishment was Priscilla Robinson, so cantankerous that local children ran at the sight of her. Prissy, as she was called, perhaps needed to be that way to run the tavern she inherited. In spite of the dire picture often presented of her, there must have been something attractive about her because she managed to catch three husbands and keep them. Some say she kept them forever.

Uncovering Some Skeletons

Sometime after Prissy died, the building was renovated to convert it from a tavern to a private home. During the renovation, six human skeletons were found buried on the property. Three of the skeletons were assumed to be Prissy's husbands who had mysteriously disappeared. The identity of the other three is lost to the ages. As far as I can tell, since the identity and age of the skeletons was never determined, they might not be her husbands. It's possible the skeletons were even there when Prissy's grandfather bought the place. Has Prissy has been maligned all these years? Is that why she won't leave her tavern?

Prissy's husbands could have just got tired of her strong personality and decided to leave. A good example of how obstinate she could be is when the new railroad was laid not far from her front door. She hated the railroad because it did not stop at the Blue Ball. Prior to the railroads, the only way of traveling was by foot or by horse. Her grandfather had purchased the Blue Ball on Old Lincoln Highway because that was the easiest and thus busiest route of traveling to and from Philadelphia. Going by rail was easier, faster, and safer than by road, so her tavern was now bypassed by the peddlers and traveling salesmen that once stopped by Prissy's place on their way down Old Lancaster Road. When the trains went by, Prissy would run out and scream curses at the rail workers. When the train hit one of her cows, her anger boiled over. She rendered the fat from the cow and coated the rails with it so the train would get stuck. It worked. The next day a representative from the railroad visited Prissy and offered her a monetary settlement for her cow.

Another interesting anecdote about Prissy appeared in the History Nook section of the Tredyffrin Historical Society Newsletter. "On her (sic) deathbed, Prissy told the undertaker that she would like to have a coffin made from Chestnut Wood so she would go through hell-a-popping."

Prissy, born in 1777, died 100 years later, in 1877, and the Blue Ball Tavern was no more. Tales of haunting began shortly after that. It is very likely that the digging up of the graves under the floor set off the haunting. The ghost could be one of those whose grave was disturbed, or it could be Prissy, perhaps returned to guard other secrets yet to be discovered. The past and present

Priscilla Robinson's Grave.

residents feel strongly that the ghost is Priscilla.

A clue that the ghost is Prissy was the incident with the Regulator Clock. The Kehlers bought an antique Regulator clock during a trip to Lancaster. The clock was just like the ones that used to hang in all the railroad stations in the 1800s. They brought it home and carefully hung the clock up on the wall. The pendulum swung a few times and then stopped. Mr. Kehler checked and double checked, but it was hung the right way. He called the dealer, who offered a few suggestions for things to check, but it was no use. The clock just wouldn't work. They returned it to the dealer, who checked it over and called them back. They returned to pick up the clock and the dealer showed them that the clock was fine and worked perfectly. They carefully took the clock back home and hung it again. It worked for a few seconds and then stopped again. The clock never worked the whole time they had it. It was among the items that were stolen when their home was burglarized. Maybe wherever it is now, it is working. The incident with the clock was what made them think their ghost was Prissy. She hated the railroad since they took business away from her and killed her calf. There was no way she would tolerate a "railroad" clock in her house.

Mr. Kehler said that he hasn't had anything happen lately, but there have been a few things over the years that just made them think. Of course, when they bought the place, they were told it was haunted, and they were told about the skeletons buried there. The skeletons aren't the only mystery of the Blue Ball. In the basement is a secret tunnel that used to connect the Blue Ball with another property. Mr. Kehler says he was told that this tunnel was probably used as part of the Underground Railroad. The Underground Railroad was at its peak from 1830 to 1865. At that time, Prissy was still firmly in control of the place.

Could this account for the skeletons found on the property? Although it's hard to believe now, Pennsylvania was right on the border of the Union and the Confederacy. Slaves that escaped to Pennsylvania had to be smuggled further north to ensure their safety. Harboring runaway slaves was illegal. Runaways would often arrive injured or sick. If they died, property owners would just have to bury them secretly. Also, if there was a secret tunnel, why would she bury the bodies under the floor?

Okay, maybe she killed so many people she ran out of space and then built a tunnel to have a place to hide the rest of the bodies. No other skeletons have ever turned up, though. "Legend has it that guests would sometimes be awakened by muffled cries in the night and scraping noises, like that of a shovel on hard dirt."1 These reports of noises were assumed to be the sounds of digging the graves. What if these were really the sounds of digging the tunnel? Were the muffled cries those of injured guests or were they slaves?

Was she a murderer or not? In addition to the rumors about travelers who checked in for the night and were never seen again, there was also a rumor about a wealthy woman who was found hung at the inn, and Prissy claimed it was suicide. Incredibly, there was an inquest into the disappearances and Prissy is reported to have said, when asked about them, "What (sic) am I supposed to do when a wine barrel falls on him while he is sleeping?" 1 Although this sounds damning, Prissy was not charged, apparently due to the lack of a corpse. Is this one of the skeletons under the floor?

What I can tell from what I have read about her, she was a headstrong woman with a tough personality who ran a rough and tumble tavern on her own. She was obviously a very independent woman who didn't take any garbage from anyone, even an inquest jury! Independent women were not very popular back then, so I am not surprised that there were ugly rumors about her.

The tunnel is what really throws a spin into this story. Although it is believed it was part of the Underground Railroad, maybe it served many purposes. It could have been used to smuggle stolen goods. Smugglers would spread stories about ghosts and hauntings in a place to keep people away, as well as to explain away odd noises like digging. Given her personality, I would say she was more likely an opportunist than a murderer, and she probably took advantage of any opportunity to make money, especially after she felt cheated by the railroad. Whether these opportunities included murder, we can only guess.

Keeping An Eye On Things...

The man the Kehlers bought the house from thought so. One day his housekeeper was alone in the house, doing some dishes in the kitchen sink. Suddenly she felt a heavy hand on her shoulder. She turned, quickly, to see an empty room behind her. Maybe it was it Prissy, the old tavern-keeper checking up on the kitchen help?

When the Kehlers moved in, one of his friends joked that he would come up one night and give him the "Prissy Knock"—a knock that consisted of a series of three quick raps. He was sitting alone one night and he heard the "Prissy Knock" at the back door. He smiled and got up to answer, anticipating a visit from his friend. When he opened the door, there was no one there.

"Is it possible he walked around to the front to play a joke on you?" I asked.

"No way," he replied, "There was snow on the ground that night and there were no footprints anywhere."

Another night, his teenage daughter was alone in the house, up in her room, doing some homework. As she sat in her bed, the door to her bedroom slowly opened. She stared at it for a second, then got up and closed it.

When she sat down again and picked up her books—"Creeeaak!" The door opened again.

Annoyed, she got up again and closed the door. With a sigh, she sat back down and picked up her books.

"Creeeaak!" she heard again and looked up to see the door slowly swinging open once more.

"That's it!" she thought. She got up, locked the door this time, and that was that.

On another occasion, when Mr. Kehler was alone in the house, he heard heavy footsteps begin heading down the stairs. He described it as sounding like someone walking in heavy, sturdy boots. The steps reached the bottom of the stairs and walked out to the kitchen. Of course, there was no one there. The footsteps were heard another time by a guest who was visiting from France. She was alone in the house when she heard the heavy boots plod across the floor above her.

I noticed a pattern to these events. They always happened when someone was alone in the house. It would be interesting to see what happened if someone who was alone in the house tried to make contact with the spirit there.

Does Prissy still watch over the Inn?

The Clockmaker's Ghost

Penn Valley—Merion, Pennsylvania

Life in 1905 was nothing like it is today. Back then, most people never traveled farther than the nearest town. Families were generally self-sufficient. They didn't have much cash, but they had clothes to wear and food to eat because they made their own necessities or bartered for what they couldn't produce. So, if you owned a clock, it was a prized possession because the average person couldn't make one. If you had a

An antique mantle clock.

clock and it stopped working, you didn't go buy another one. You got someone to fix it. There were always traveling peddlers and repairmen looking for work.

In 1905, a clock repairman named William Crossley was returning home to Germantown from the Narberth home of Mrs. DuBosq. He had repaired her clock for $1. It was a hot July day when he passed by a cool spring on the Hoehler farm in Penn Valley. Thinking a cool drink would be refreshing, he stopped. It was the death of him.

Suicide or Murder?

Two gunshots destroyed the peace of that sultry summer day. Farmer Augustus Hoehler, Mrs. Hoehler, and their daughter, Cora, ran towards the direction the shots came from. They saw two men running away and William Crossley lying on the ground next to the spring in a pool of blood. He had been shot twice in the face. A person who had been gathering herbs in the area that day also heard the shots and saw two men fleeing.

Coroner William R. Devitt was called to the scene. Instead of launching a manhunt for the two suspects, he expressed great displeasure at having had to travel the thirty miles down the hot and dusty road to the farm. "Suicide!" he pronounced, and then set off back towards his home on Green Lane.

Apparently, Police Chief Ike Chambers took his job more seriously. He noticed right away that Mr. Crossley's repair kit, which had contained a number of gold and silver watches, had been forced open. The watches were gone and so were his earnings. A tenant of one of the "Keech stone cottages" on Hollow Road was questioned but no one was ever arrested. Disregarding the evidence collected by Chief Chambers, the coroner's jury supported Devitt's finding of suicide.

"If it was suicide," asked Chief Chambers, "what the heck happened to the gun?" No gun had ever turned up at the scene or even nearby.

Please Help Me...

Shortly after the suicide verdict, travelers reported hearing and seeing the sad ghost of William Crossley. He was walking in the woods of Penn Valley along Centennial Road and Conshohocken State Road, moaning and crying out. Some think he was looking for vengeance. Others think he just wanted someone to hear his side of the story.

Lonely Centennial Road – No sign of the forest that was once there.

On September 14, 1944, The Great Atlantic Hurricane came through, pouring about six inches of rain and tearing up many of the trees in the haunted woods along Centennial Road. The sad clockmaker ghost wasn't seen as much after that.

The area where the clockmaker was murdered looks a lot different nearly a century later. There are no more farms here, and no sign of the spring where he stopped for refreshment. Has the ghost disappeared with the woods?

A Talk With the Ghost

We had trouble finding Centennial Road the first few times we went looking for it. The third time, armed with a map, we located the street. It was difficult to see the street sign in the dusk, and although it was a pleasant evening and we had passed many walkers on the way, Centennial Road appeared to be deserted. When I started to walk down the road, I concentrated on Mr. Crossley and wondered where along the road he might appear.

About halfway down the road, it seemed to get suddenly quiet, as if I were suddenly suspended in time somewhere. I turned quickly to look behind me and caught a flash of something. I took a photo and paused for a moment, watching.

I began walking again. That eerie feeling was still with me, so I glanced over my shoulder often, hoping to see whatever was behind me. After I got half a block down, I decided to confront whoever or whatever it was. "William Crossley?" I called into the darkening dusk. "Is that you?" I received no answer from the darkness that swallowed up the road, so I decided to take one last photo. As I took it, I said, "William, I know you didn't kill yourself. I am writing about what happened to you here and I am going to tell the truth; that you were robbed and murdered. I'd really love to have a picture of you to go with it." Here's the photo I took:

Is that you, William?

Haunts of Penn Valley

Penn Valley in Lower Merion –
Marked by these signs and many haunted locations.

The Haunted Woods at Gulley Run

I t's a nice park now, but when Gulley Run was known as Bowler's Woods, the area was feared and avoided by the local children. It was very haunted. The woods were full of smoky mists, shadowy forms, and moaning specters, as well as gnomes, goblins, and trolls. Gerry Francis of the Lower Merion Historical Society blames the nearby Belmont Driving Park for the haunting of Bowler's Woods. "When they built the driving park, it attracted crowds of people," he explained. "Gypsies and hoboes would camp in the woods, near the park where they made their living working the crowds. If someone got too close to their camp site, they would make noises to scare them off. The smoky mist was smoke from their campfires."

A first-person account of the haunted woods, told by Mrs. George T. Grow, appeared in the October 27, 1976 issue of *Main Line Times*. Mrs. Grow had lived her whole life in Penn Valley. She told this story shortly before she died at the age of 101. She remembered "hearing …strange sounds and reports of spectral lights in Bowlers Woods" when she was a little girl.

The stories of the ghosts in the woods were probably encouraged by parents who would likely have wanted their children to steer as far clear of the woods as possible.

Murder Orchard

Was it murder or suicide that created the ghost of Murder Orchard? Accounts differ as to the cause, but the manner of death is the same in all accounts. A man was found hanging from one of the trees here. From that day on, his ghost was seen in the vicinity of the orchard; always with a noose around his neck.

The haunted Bowler's Woods at Gulley Run.

All that remains of Murder Orchard.

Today the orchard is gone. Where the orchard used to be is behind the Staples on Montgomery Avenue. Although I dismissed this story as just legend, when I went there at night, I did not want to get out of my car and I noticed that although there are quite a few shops near there, the back parking lot was strangely deserted. There was definitely a disquieting presence in that area that makes one reluctant to linger.

Rathalla

and the Revenants of Rosemont

A House Built by Spirits

O f course, the spirits that helped build Rathalla came in a bottle from a distillery. Joseph Francis Sinnott had started out in 1854 as a seventeen-year-old Irish immigrant in Philadelphia. Two years later, he was an assistant bookkeeper at John Gibson's Son & Company distillery. He took a brief break to defend the Union in the Civil War, but by 1861, he had returned to Gibson's, where he was put in charge of opening a branch in Boston.

In 1863, he married Annie Rogers, whom he had met in Philadelphia, and they moved to Boston. Three years later, they were on their way back to Philadelphia so Joseph could take up a position as partner at Gibson's. In 1884, when Gibson retired, Joseph Sinnott and another man, Andrew Moore, took over the running of the business. Upon Moore's death in 1888, Sinnott was able to step in as owner of the company.

The next year, 1889, Sinnott bought a large parcel of property in what was then Rosemont Farms. In time for the summer season of 1891, his castle was ready. Rathalla is an impressive gray stone structure complete with towers and gargoyles, meant to impress passersby from its place atop a gentle rise on Montgomery Avenue.

Rathalla was chosen as the name of this Main Line country home. According to the Lower Merion Historical Society records, the name means "home of the chieftain upon the highest hill" in Gaelic. According to a booklet about Rathalla

A house fit for a chieftain.

written by Rosemont alum Margaretta Richardi, two other names were discussed first. Mrs. Sinnott wanted to call the house "Agincourt," after a French castle that was likely imaginary, since the real castle near the battle of Agincourt has been in ruins since the castle near Agincourt, or Azincourt as it is properly called, was in a ruin at least a century before Rathalla was even conceived. Rathalla more resembles Beauvais at Azay or Montresor. Joseph's brother, Father James, suggested it be called "Rum Done It." He also pointed out that "Agincourt" could easily be "A Gin Court," so the name Rathalla, which in Gaelic means (as mentioned before) "the house of the chieftain upon the high hill," was selected.

The mansion was just as impressive on the inside. There was plenty of room for Mr. Sinnott, his wife, and their nine

The dining room at Rathalla.

children. Mr. Sinnott died in 1906, and his wife died in 1918. The mansion stood empty after Mrs. Sinnott's death until 1921, when it was purchased by the Sisters of the Holy Child, who started Rosemont College, a Catholic Women's College. Rathalla was so big it contained the classrooms, dormitories, chapel, and dining hall. The Sisters also still lived there.

What About the Ghosts?

I was not able to discover why Rathalla is haunted or who haunts it, but I have heard the same reports from people who didn't know each other. The most compelling reports were from a plumber who was restoring the plumbing in 2000. He was a friend of mine who knew I was interested in the paranormal, so he told me that I would love the place he was working on. As he was working, he would constantly hear the sound of children playing, laughing, and running on the porch.

After the first couple of days, he stopped checking to see who it was because there was never anyone there. He even got to the point of leaving a tape recorder running to try and capture the sound. He would hear the children, and when the sounds faded, he would go over to the tape recorder. There was never anything recorded.

He also heard the sounds of someone working in the basement. In the beginning, he heard the digging and sawing noises coming from below and he went to see who else was there. When he opened the basement door, the noise instantly cut off and he found himself peering down into complete darkness. He was never able to work up the courage to go down there, though.

At first he wouldn't tell me where the place was. It was owned by a Catholic Church order and he was afraid of causing problems if anyone went up there. As he described the building, though, I couldn't help but recall that it sounded exactly like what a friend of my grandmother's told me she'd experienced as a student at Rosemont College. I asked him if it was Rosemont and his face told me all I needed to know.

The sound of children playing is heard coming from this porch.

"How did you know that?" he asked in shock. I knew he was really impressed with my psychic abilities, so I had to admit that I had heard the exact same story from my grandmother's friend who had attended classes there. There was one additional event in her story, though.

She was describing the impressive main hall of the mansion and describing the beautiful woodwork and windows. The first time she went in there she said she was awestruck by the sheer beauty of the place. She had walked over to the main staircase and placed her hand on the carved newel post when she said her "blood literally ran cold." She said she never understood what that expression meant until that very moment. She said she was certain there was some kind of negative presence there. She reported the children and the sounds of work in the basement. The Sisters said they didn't hear anything.

Thinking it was possible these people were sensitive and picking up on vibrations from the house, I decided a trip to Rathalla was what was needed to clear things up. Research into the history of the Sinnott family turned up no tragedies involving young children. The only people who died there were Mr. and Mrs. Sinnott and their eldest son, Joseph Edward, who died in 1892. I was curious to see what would happen when I got there.

The house is remarkable. There are gargoyles and carvings everywhere. I didn't feel or hear anything unusual while we were there, and we sat in the living room for over an hour. It was very quiet and seemed tranquil. The main staircase didn't give me a cold feeling at all. A walk around the building didn't provide any more insight. The only explanation I can provide for what my witnesses experienced was that my grandmother's friend had her experience a very long time ago, in the early days of the college. Whatever caused the phenomena she experienced could have moved on or been depleted until it was disrupted or re-energized during the extensive renovations that were done in 2000. Another possibility is that I wasn't there at the right time to experience the phenomena. We will have to wait and see if anyone else comes forward with an experience they had there.

A Lost Boy
at a Bryn Mawr Mansion

Bryn Mawr, Pennsylvania

I magine you are a building contractor. You have been hired to help convert an old estate into a new residential treatment center. It's a big job and you have a deadline. Everything is going well until one day, two of your workers won't stay after dark. Tools keep disappearing. Wires are pulled out of the walls after you put them in. Is there someone sabotaging your building site? The thought crosses your mind and you are about to look into hiring security when your phone rings. It is one of the workers who left early today.

"I don't want you to be mad at me, but I can't stay there after dark anymore," says the worker.

"Not you, too!" exclaims the contractor in exasperation.

"Look, that place is creepy, explains the workman, "I saw something today I never want to see again. I don't even know if I can talk about it."

"I understand," sighed the boss, defeated. The call disconnected. "How the heck am I going to get this job done on time?" He envisioned a long series of late nights there alone. He had to admit, the thought was not a comforting one. He wasn't comfortable there, either, but he had a contract to fulfill.

When he first got the job, he had been looking forward to it. He loved working on big, old mansions. They had so many interesting architectural features and it was always a challenge trying to figure out the best way to convert them for modern uses. This one was going to be a treatment center. There was a big main house that was going to be converted into dormitories with a nursing center and a dining hall. Another smaller building was to be converted into offices and a conference center, and a carriage house that was also being updated for some future use. There were several other houses on the estate grounds, although when he was hired to work on it, most of the outbuildings had fallen down.

This one turned into a bigger challenge than expected. There were doors slamming constantly. When he went to check, there was no one there. Tools disappeared, resulting in arguments and accusations between workers. The latest development was that they all seemed to be finding excuses for leaving early. He felt like there was something there; he'd heard the doors slam, his tools vanished when he put them down, and he had photos of the building that contained large glowing orbs and misty shapes.

By the end of the week, he realized that he was going to be finishing the job himself. He never saw a darn thing the whole time. He heard things and felt a presence, but never saw one thing, not even a shadow out of the corner of his eye.

When he was finally done with the job, he called the workman who had said he saw something there. He still didn't want to talk about it because it had given him nightmares for days afterward, but he finally talked. He had been up on a ladder working on some phone wire when he felt something tugging at it. He looked down, thinking it had caught a nail or something. There was a little boy standing there, looking up at him. He had to grip the ladder to keep from falling off and crying out. This was no ordinary little kid. He described the little boy as "unnatural... his skin was the color of the underside of a rotten fish." The whole encounter had lasted seconds, but it was long enough to convince him that he had no business being there.

The Haunted Mansion at Cabrini

Radnor, Pennsylvania

C abrini College looks haunted. To enter from King of Prussia Road, drive through the iron entrance gates and past an Elizabethan-style gatehouse. Continue on up a winding, tree-lined lane to the campus. To enter from the other side of campus, drive up their tree-lined arcade to a Tudor-style building that used to be the stables. The business offices are in the old Dorrance mansion and the registrar is in the old stables. There are carvings of gargoyles all over the place to give it an even more gothic atmosphere.

The mansion, known as Woodcrest, was completed in 1902 for James W. Paul, Jr. and his family. His wife, Frances (Fanny) Drexel, died ten years earlier and he wanted to build a nice country home for his children. He lived there with his two daughters, Ellen and Mary, and his son, Anthony Joseph. When Ellen married Paul Mills in 1903, Woodcrest was described in the *New York Times* society page as "one of the most picturesque houses in the country." James Paul died in 1908, but the family kept the mansion until 1925, when Mary Paul Munn, his younger daughter, sold the mansion to Mr. John T. Dorrance. Mr. Dorrance was the president of the Campbell's Soup Company and Woodcrest was going to be his family's new Main Line home. John Dorrance had four daughters and one son. Tradition is that the ghosts of Cabrini College are from the time of the Dorrances' ownership.

Gargoyles watch over the main entrance at Woodcrest.

Star-Crossed Lovers

The story is that one of the Dorrance daughters became very friendly with one of the stable boys. When her father found out, he forbade them to see each other. Of course, she

**The roadway between the former stables and the Mansion –
Where the man in black is seen.**

continued seeing him anyway and became pregnant. At this point, the story goes in different directions. In one version, when Mr. Dorrance discovered the pregnancy, he marched out in the snow to confront the stable boy. The stable boy had already hung himself, and Dr. Dorrance found the body. When the daughter heard about her lover's suicide, in typical Romeo and Juliet fashion, she jumped off the balcony of the mansion and fell to her death.

In another version, the girl hid the pregnancy from her family. She went into premature labor and the baby was stillborn. In an alternate version, the pregnancy was discovered when she went into labor and the baby was taken from her and smothered. In both of these versions, the baby was buried in the apple orchard. Woodcrest Dorm is said to occupy the space that was formerly the apple orchard.

In all versions, the girl is now seen wandering the mansion and the campus, wearing a blue dress and searching for her baby. She has even been said to ask people if they have seen her baby. A man believed to be Mr. Dorrance is seen walking between the mansion and the stable.

Giving up the Ghosts

In an interesting twist, an article published in the October 28, 2004 issue of the *Loquitor*, Cabrini's campus newspaper, claims that an unnamed group of girls from the class of 1966 made the whole thing up to entertain themselves one Saturday night. They are said to have admitted this at their 35th reunion in 2001. The problem I have with this article is that it contains so many errors, it is difficult to believe anything in it. Also, there are those continuous reports of the ghost of a young girl in a blue dress and the man in black. The sightings of the girl are always in the Woodcrest dorm, the mansion, and the grounds between them. The man is always seen walking between Grace Hall, formerly the stables, and the Mansion.

In another *Loquitor* article, published on October 28, 2005, Martha Dale, the coordinator of historical exhibits for the 50th anniversary of the Mansion at Cabrini, said, "I don't know of anything in particular that happened at Woodcrest that might have given rise to our ghost stories. It's important to emphasize (sic) that they have no basis in fact as far as we know." Dale added, "We are in touch with both the Paul family and the Dorrance (sic) family, and all their daughters are accounted for!" The article continues on, stating that "The Dorrances' (sic) had two daughters who are both accounted for in records." This statement, according available records, appears to be false. Census records for 1910 and 1920 show that the Dorrances had four daughters; Elinor, Ethel, Charlotte, and Margaret. When the Dorrances purchased the house in 1925, Elinor was eighteen and Ethel was sixteen. Elinor may have been married and not living at home, but the other three daughters likely spent at least some time there. The Dorrances were frequent world travelers and also owned a house in New Jersey which is the house listed as their primary residence in the census records.

The Dorrance Family

Research on the Dorrance family shows that Mr. Dorrance died in 1930. At that time, their youngest daughter, Margaret, was fifteen years old. Another daughter, Charlotte, was nineteen. Their son, John, was only eleven. Could Mr. Dorrance be returning to the estate to check on his youngest children?

When Mr. Dorrance died, there was a huge dispute between the states of Pennsylvania and New Jersey over which state had the rights to his inheritance taxes, which amounted to about $15 million. In 1934, the inheritance tax was paid to Pennsylvania, but according to an article in the July 4, 2008 issue of *TIME* magazine, the state of New Jersey just took a check from the estate for about $15.5 million. The Supreme Court refused to rehear the case and the result was the first ever double death tax, in which two states got to tax the estate of a deceased person. If you ask me, that is enough to make Mr. Dorrance haunt the place. Maybe he is trying to let everyone know where his home really was.

The only realistic candidate for the ghost from the Dorrance family is the elusive Margaret, the youngest daughter. Margaret traveled to Bermuda in April of 1931, eight months after her father's death. Her return to the U.S. is recorded in immigration records for that year. She traveled there again in 1934 when she was nineteen, and her return to the United States was recorded again. After that, I could locate no record of her. It is possible that she got married and her name changed, but all of her sibling's marriages, name changes, and deaths are well-documented. Her absence from public records could also be explained if she relocated to a foreign country, but it is odd that all mention of her disappears after 1934. It's even possible that she is still alive, as well, but I have not been able to find any mention of her after her return from Bermuda in 1934. Back then, they only recorded when people came into the United States, not when they left it.

Woodcrest was owned by the Dorrance family until 1953, when it was sold to the Missionary Sisters of the Sacred Heart of Jesus. They turned the Mansion into the Villa Cabrini orphanage and it was the home of seventy-two orphans according to Cabrini literature, until 1957 when Sister Ursula Infante opened Cabrini College and the Mansion became offices and dormitories. At that time, the female college students moved into Woodcrest, which they shared with the nuns and the orphans.

I attended Cabrini College from 2004 to 2007, and every fall and winter would be marked by a rash of ghost sightings. Most of the sightings I heard were of the man in black that hurried along the path between the Mansion and Grace Hall. In each report, he seemed to come out of nowhere, wearing a dark suit in the style of the early 1900s. The reports have caused me to re-examine the evidence for the ghost being that of Mr. Dorrance. From the descriptions of the man, it sounds more like Mr. Paul, who lived there in the early 1900s. The Paul family did use Woodcrest as their primary residence and often entertained there in the lavish style of the times, holding many formal dress events on the property.

The Haunted Mansion

My mother attended Cabrini College in the 1970s. At that time, there were still dormitory rooms in the mansion. She said they were reserved for seniors and everyone wanted to get a room assignment there. The first ghost story I heard about Cabrini came from this time. A girl whose dorm room was in the mansion was expecting her mother to come to visit her. She left her dorm room unlocked because her mother would probably get there while she was still in class. Her mother arrived and walked into her room. She knew her daughter wouldn't be back for a couple of hours, so she decided to lie down on the bed and take a quick nap. She woke to the sound of footsteps approaching the bed and quickly turned over to greet her daughter. There was no one there. A few minutes later, when the daughter arrived, she found her mother very shaken and anxious to leave. The mom didn't want to tell what happened for fear of scaring her daughter, but the story was coaxed out of her. The daughter wasn't scared at all; in fact she had experienced similar things in her room. She said she had never felt threatened by it, so she just accepted it as part of living in an old mansion.

Other students have reported seeing a girl in a blue dress wandering the grounds in the areas around Woodcrest Dorm and the Woodcrest Mansion. Some of the employees in the Mansion offices have admitted they felt what they described as a "ghostly presence," but felt it was a friendly presence, similar to the feeling of the former student who heard footsteps in her Mansion dorm room—"it comes with being in a place this old."

I had two experiences with the ghost in the mansion. The first was when I was trying to register for classes for the first time. I had been told that my advisor's office was in the Mansion. Not realizing how massive the mansion was, I set off down an upstairs hallway in search of the office number and was quickly lost in a maze of hallways. Since it was summer and between regular registration and the start of the semester, they weren't many people there and I couldn't find anyone to ask directions. Then at the end of a hallway I saw a flash of white that looked like a woman in a white dress. I took off after her, calling, "Excuse me, I'm lost...", rounded the corner and came to a dead end. There were no stairs and all I could see were two closed office doors. Assuming she had gone into one of them, I walked up to the first office door and knocked on it and when there was no answer I moved to the next door. The name of my advisor was on the door, but it was locked and there was no answer. I went back to the first door and tried the knob. It was locked. So who did I see?

At this point, I had heard vague rumors about the mansion being haunted, so after another quick look around to make sure there was no way anyone could have gone in or out without being seen, I went back the way I came, glancing behind me every once in a while to see if there was anyone there. I wondered if the ghost had helped me to find the room I was looking for. If so, it's a shame she didn't stick around long enough for me to thank her. Since my days at Cabrini were just starting, I was hoping to get the chance to thank her in the future.

The second experience I had there was on another trip to my advisor's office. I was hoping to catch her before the semester ended for winter break because I had some questions about a class I needed. She wasn't in her office, but there was a bulletin board we could leave notes on. I dug through my handbag but could not find a piece of paper, so I decided to see if there was anyone down the hall in one of the offices who could give me something to write on. As I rounded the corner, I heard footsteps behind me. I turned quickly to see what or who it was, since I knew I had just come from a dead end hallway, but there was no one there. The place I stopped was right in front of a window. As I looked around and my glance fell on the window, I saw a flash of something behind me reflected in the glass. Again, I turned quickly but there was nothing there. Thinking it must be her, I said, "Thank you for helping me find the office the day I was lost!" I hope she heard me.

The final strange experience I had at the Mansion was when my family accompanied me to an honors reception held there. There were about thirty other people attending besides us, so it wasn't too crowded. The reception was held in the main hall area of the mansion, under the balcony the girl is said to have thrown herself from in some versions of the legend. My daughters were with me that day. I hadn't told them anything about the ghosts because I didn't want to scare them, so I was surprised when my youngest daughter came up and asked me if this house was haunted.

Assuming that her sisters had tried to scare her, I asked her why. She then told me that she had seen a girl in a white dress come down the main staircase and then when she got halfway across the room, she disappeared. She said she was watching her because she was dressed so fancy, like a bride or something. When the girl disappeared, she thought it might be a ghost.

"Well," I said to her, "some people think this house is haunted." She looked up at me and said, "Well, Mommy, you need to tell them it *is* haunted because I saw the ghost!"

Now I have my chance to tell what she saw there that evening, so here it is.

The Haunted Mansion at Cabrini

Woodcrest Mansion's main staircase – Always an active spot.

So who is the girl? I was beginning to think there was more than one female ghost. The one that I saw certainly didn't seem like a gliding girl in blue or a girl in a formal dress. My impression was more that of a servant. The girl that has been described outside is said to be clothed in a blue dress, not a white one. My daughter was positive the girl she saw was wearing white. Perhaps there are three ghosts—the one in blue that is looking for her baby, the servant on the upper floor hallway, and the girl in fancy dress who likes parties.

Who are these ghostly Cabrini girls? After extensive research, it is impossible to say. The Paul family's household included at least five female servants. The Dorrances surely had an equal number. One possibility for the girl in blue that I have not heard advanced is that she could have been one of the orphans from the time it was an orphanage. She could be searching for her baby doll or even a baby brother or sister. The girl in the pretty party dress that my daughter saw could be a Paul or a Dorrance. The Pauls entertained there often, so my feeling is that the ghost is a Paul. In a May 1921 issue of *Country Life* magazine, Woodcrest appeared in an ad that read a "gentleman going abroad desires to let his country place, furnished, for low rental". I could find no record of whether it was rented or not. If it was, the origin of the ghost could be from that time. Whoever she is, she certainly picked a beautiful place to spend her afterlife.

A Deadly Love Triangle at the Old McGeorge Mansion

Bala Cynwyd, Pennsylvania

No castle or mansion is complete without its ghostly "lady." There's the famous Brown Lady of Raynham Hall in Norfolk, England. Pevensey Castle in Sussex, England, has the "pale lady." Skipness and Crathes Castles in Scotland and Caerphilly in Wales have their green ladies, Avenel Plantation in Virginia has its "white lady," and the old McGeorge Mansion in Merion, Pennsylvania has the "grey lady." Well, the grey lady used to have a mansion. It was demolished in 1934. For years, local children played in the ruins. Today, the land where the mansion once stood is occupied by the Merion Court Apartments.

The reports of the ghostly grey lady were so frequent and vivid that they attracted the attention of the Pennsylvania Historical Society. The Historical Society then requested that the Society for Psychical Research to investigate. Agents of the Society did so, and pronounced the place to be a genuine haunted house!

Sightings of the grey lady were a common occurrence for members of the McGeorge family. A granddaughter of Mr. McGeorge, Miss Wilmot Schoff, saw the lady ghost and publicly admitted that it terrified her. "It was several years ago," she is quoted as saying in the *Milwaukee Journal*. "I was coming up the back stairs and turning a corner at the second floor. I saw her standing there! It was in the middle of the day…I screamed and ran downstairs…"

She has appeared at all hours of the day. On another occasion, the grey lady appeared to Mrs. McGeorge as she was seated at the table eating breakfast. Mrs. McGeorge saw her pass by and got up to see where she was going. The ghost entered the library and sat down. When she spoke to the grey lady, the ghost faded and then vanished. Mrs. McGeorge described her as being dressed in a Civil War-era gown and wearing a shawl that was fastened with a brooch.

The ghost was also heard singing and playing the piano. Witnesses report that the ghost exhibited great musical talent. Perhaps she was playing and singing for the other resident ghost, the Colonel.

The grey lady isn't spending her afterlife alone. The Colonel, generally believed to be her husband, was also sighted in the house and walking the grounds of the beautiful estate. Sadly, I can find no record of who they were! All records I have discovered begin in the late 1800s and refer to the house as the "McGeorge Mansion." The mansion is mentioned in a book published in 1897, and described as "Mr. McGeorge's place (called The Highlands) … seen on the hill on Montgomery Avenue."[1] According to property and census records, it was owned and lived in by this same McGeorge family until it was demolished.

So Who is the Colonel?

William McGeorge, a lawyer, first appears in Philadelphia records in 1870. It is unlikely that he and his wife, Mary Armadelle Clark, are the ghosts because there is no mention of Mr. McGeorge having served in the military or in the Civil War. Their son, Percy, was born in 1865 in New York. It is likely, then, that they relocated to Philadelphia and purchased the mansion around 1870, when they first appear in the census records for Philadelphia.

In the search for a possible name for our grey lady and her Colonel, I looked for earlier references to the property. The only clue as to when the mansion was built is that it's said that the columns at the front of the McGeorge Mansion were taken from Morris' folly in Philadelphia.

Robert Morris was the financier of the American Revolution whose wealth came mainly from privateering and lucky investments. Although he was successful in securing financing for the Revolution, he was not able to sustain his own personal financial success and only four years after beginning construction on his mansion in Philadelphia, he ended up in prison for debt. His unfinished mansion, which became known as "Morris' Folly," was sold for parts in 1801. The columns ended up on "The Highlands" in Bala Cynwyd, so it follows that the grey lady's home was being built around that time. Perhaps they brought some of the anguish of Morris with them to this new property. The only other reference I could find was with this old photo from 1888, when Mr. McGeorge hired architect T.P. Chandler to alter the mansion known as "The Highlands" in 1888.

The story of the grey lady starts off well enough. A young Colonel in the Union Army took his pretty young wife to this stately mansion which was to be her home. He gallantly went off to war, vowing to return to his new wife as soon as he could. The young wife was lonely and soon began an affair with a local doctor. When the Colonel was wounded, he got a furlough and decided to come home and surprise his young bride. When he reached his home, he quietly entered the house and crept up to their bedroom, where instead of welcoming arms, he finds his wife in bed with her lover. The Colonel murdered the lover and concealed the body in the basement wall of the house. Distraught, the

Colonel then left the house. It is the last that was heard of him.

Together Forever?

The Colonel never returned to his home or his wife. After the initial shock wore off, the wife began to dress in mourning grey clothes and spent the rest of her life roaming the house. Some say she was mourning her lost lover. I think that she may have been performing some kind of penance. Before too long, she wasted away from grief and remorse, and died.

It is not clear why the Colonel, who refused to return to the mansion in life, would do so after death, but his ghost was seen there during the time of the McGeorge's ownership. Did he try to reconcile with his wife after death? He was not seen after the mansion was torn down, but his

Which part of the Mansion was here?

Low sobbing can be heard by the pathway behind the apartments.

sad wife, the grey lady, has been seen roaming the area. Maybe the Colonel gave up. It's possible that she was so wrapped up in her own grief that she didn't see anything but that, or perhaps she is still watching over the burial place of her lover.

There was no report of a skeleton found in 1934 when the house was razed. So either it is still there under the apartment complex or it was never there. If you see the grey lady, ask her what really happened. Maybe when she tells her story to someone, she will be able to leave this place where she made the mistake of forming a deadly love triangle.

A Lingering Sadness

The Merion Court Apartments was a quiet and peaceful little spot when we stopped there to look for the grey lady. As we walked down the path behind the buildings, I wondered what part of the house had been at this location.

"Wait a minute," I said to my daughter, Aarika, as we paused on the walkway, "Do you hear that?"

"What?" she asked.

"Crying," I answered. We stood silently, listening. I could hear the traffic, snatches of conversation, and underneath it all, I heard this low, steady, heartbreaking sobbing. I looked over at Aarika. It was obvious she wasn't hearing it. As we stood there looking at each other, a sodium light at the corner of one of the buildings started buzzing and then popped loudly. "Maybe we should go that way," I said, pointing towards the steps under the light.

The steps led to a shady, quiet courtyard that must have given the Merion Court Apartments their name. This must have been the heart of the old mansion. The steady sobbing was still there, not louder or fainter, but just as if it had stayed with us. Was it the gray lady? I can't be sure.

Nothing unusual showed up in any of the photos. More interesting is that the crying that I heard didn't show up on the audio recording.

As we turned out of the parking lot, I couldn't help but glance over at the courtyard. It was so shady and full of shadows that a passerby would never notice one small grey shadow among many. If one listens, however, the low sobbing of a lonely soul may still be heard.

Westminster Cemetery—
The Hitchhiking Ghost

Bala Cynwyd, Pennsylvania

T he same year the McGeorge Mansion was torn down, stories began to circulate about a ghostly female hitchhiker near Westminster Cemetery. The story got so big that local police had to chase groups of people out of the cemetery, where they had gathered at night to try and catch a glimpse of the hitchhiking ghost of Westminster Cemetery.

The story is a familiar one. On bright, moonlit nights, people driving past the Westminster Cemetery on Belmont Avenue would see a young woman hitchhiking. When the driver stops and rolls down the window, she asks the driver for a ride to her home in Germantown. When they arrive at the address, the driver goes to let her out only to find that she has vanished.

Unfortunately, I could find no reports of first hand sightings of this ghost. In the 1930s, there was an explosion of reports of hitchhiking ghosts all over the United States. The basic story is the same with some local variation. The most famous of these hitchhiker ghosts is probably Resurrection Mary in Chicago. Of course, there are witnesses who claim to have actually seen Resurrection Mary, standing by the side of Archer Avenue outside the old Resurrection Cemetery.

This urban legend of the vanishing hitchhiker predates automobiles and was first recorded around 1900 in the United States. "It acquired the automobile motif by the period of the

Is this where the Phantom Hitchhiker walks?

Great Depression, and thereafter spawned a number of subtypes with greatly varied and oddly interlocking details.[1]

According to Jerry Francis of the Lower Merion Historical Society, Westminster Cemetery was where you were buried if you were middle class. Wealthy and famous people were buried in West

Laurel Hill. Despite this generalization, there are some very large and elaborate mausoleums in Westminster Cemetery with beautiful stained glass and statuary. But does it have any ghosts?

During my research for this book, I traveled up and down Belmont Avenue past the cemetery many times. I have never seen the hitchhiking ghost or felt a presence by the roadside. Just inside the gates, however is a different story. To the left as you enter the cemetery is a very creepy-looking and feeling lagoon. My initial feelings about the lagoon were confirmed on a subsequent visit with two other people, who, without prompting both told me they felt there was "something spooky" about the lagoon.

We decided to have a session with our "ghost box" near the lagoon to see if we could find out anything from the spirits themselves.

A "ghost box" is basically a digital radio that is modified so that it scans the stations continuously. Many paranormal investigators believe that ghosts and spirits can then speak through this modified radio. Since the start of our experiments with the box, we have received many messages that were positive and enlightening. The session that day at Westminster is available on line at: http://www.youtube.com/watch?v=vjZekqlRaDo.

During the session, we made contact with a spirit named Steve and a female spirit that we called Ms. X because she declined to provide her name. We asked Steve if there was a hitchhiking ghost outside the cemetery. He said, "No." We further asked if he has ever seen her there, to which he also replied, "No." To confirm all of this I then asked, "So it is just a legend? It was all made up then?" to which he replied, "Yes." We further asked if the cemetery was haunted and the voice said, "No," but when we asked him if he stayed in the lagoon area he said, "Yes," indicating that there is at least one spirit that frequents the Westminster Cemetery, and it is not the hitchhiker ghost!

Westminster's creepy lagoon.

There were a couple of other things that we experienced during our visit to Westminster. The first thing involved my car. When I left the house, the fuel gauge was at half of a tank. The cemetery is only about ten miles from my house, so when I pulled into the gates and saw the "empty" signal flash, I assumed it was a short or something wrong with the gauge. After the ghost box session, I pulled out onto Belmont Avenue to look for a gas station. As soon as I got onto the road, the gauge went back to almost half a tank. Again, I thought maybe the gauge was broken, but it has been fine ever since. So if you go to Westminster Cemetery, make sure you have a full tank of gas!

The other thing that happened involved my sixteen-year-old daughter who had accompanied me on this trip. She had a scrape on her leg that she'd gotten while riding her bike a couple days before. As we drove down Belmont Avenue on our way home, she told me that her scrape ached the whole time we were in the cemetery, but it felt better now. She tried putting weight on her foot and turning her leg. The only thing that made it feel like that, she found, was application of direct pressure to the wound.

Was the ghost at the lagoon playing with us to get our attention? The evidence points in that direction. When I posted the ghost box video on youtube.com, one user heard a voice ask, "Will she help us?" She felt that the voices on the recording wanted help with moving on to the light. At the end of each session, I encourage any ghost that is present to join loved ones that are waiting for them. Maybe that's why the gauge righted itself and the pressure on my daughter's leg stopped. Perhaps the spirits had moved on.

Another Roadside Ghost

Hanging Rock on Route 320

No, there are no gallows here and no one was hanged. Instead, the spirit of a young woman with long hair has been seen gliding across the road. She is believed to be the ghost of a camp follower. Washington's troops camped near the rock during the Revolution.

A Haunting Presence

A Private Home in Bryn Mawr, Pennsylvania

G race was so excited about the house! It was in a great location, reasonably priced, and had plenty of room for her two sons. She couldn't believe it was still available. When she told her husband about it, he drove by the place with her that night.

"Isn't it great?" she asked.

"It's definitely bigger than where we are now," he answered. There was something in his voice...

"What's wrong? You don't like it?" asked Grace. She was so sure it was perfect. Why couldn't he see it?

"Well it's really overgrown and..."

"And?" she prompted.

"Don't you think it looks kind of creepy?"

"Oh my God!" she cried, "That's just because it's dark. I think it's been vacant for a while. All it needs is some cleaning up and trimming!"

Her husband was silent.

"Come on, honey," she pleaded, "I am so sick of living on top of each other. We can afford this! Look at all the rose bushes; this place is going to be gorgeous in the spring."

"All right," he said, "since you're so in love with it..."

Grace went to sleep smiling that night. She was already dreaming about where she would put their things.

She was so excited, she didn't even mind packing. The week before they moved in, Grace convinced one of her friends to help her do some cleaning at the new house to get it ready. Her friend, Sean, didn't need much convincing; he had heard so much about the place by now he couldn't wait to see it. They went in and she gave him the grand tour. As they went up onto the third floor, he remarked, "Wow! It's really cold up here. There must be no insulation or something."

It was cold up there. She had noticed it before when they had first gone through the house. Sean shivered and rubbed his arms. "Aren't top floors supposed to be hotter?" They both looked at the sunlight streaming in through the windows. "It's probably just a draft," said Grace, as she looked out the window at the calm, still trees, "You know how old houses are. We have a lot of work to do so we better get started."

What the...?

They did some general cleaning and after their lunch break Grace decided to cut some of the hedges and rose bushes back from the front walk. "That should cheer things up and make it a lot easier to move things in!" she thought to herself. The house seemed so dark inside. There were no curtains on the windows yet, so she attributed the darkness to the wildly overgrown landscape that surrounded the house.

She went to get her gardening tools and the electric hedge trimmer out of the car. Walking into the kitchen, she set the box of tools on the floor and looked for an outlet to plug in the trimmer. She tried to open the window so she could put the cord in through, but it wouldn't budge. Putting the trimmer down, she went to find Sean. He was on the third floor, examining a black stain that was on the wall all around the heating vent.

"Sean," she started.

"Aahh!" he yelled and jumped, "You scared the crap out of me!"

"I need help with a window." said Grace.

"Oh, okay. Let's go. I don't know how we are going to get that off," he said, pointing to the stain.

"Maybe it doesn't come off," joked Grace, laughing, "Maybe that's where the ghosts come in and out!" Both laughing now, they went down the stairs to the kitchen.

They entered the kitchen and Sean almost walked into her when she stopped short. "What the…?" exclaimed Grace.

"What?" wondered Sean.

"My garden toolbox. It's gone! I left it right here," she stated, pointing at the floor. The trimmer was still there.

"Nah, you probably didn't realize you were carrying it and put it down somewhere in the house when you were looking for me," explained Sean.

"Maybe," she replied. She didn't feel convinced, though. She knew she'd put them there.

They plugged in the trimmer and got to work clearing the front path. One dusty, dirty hour later they were almost finished. Sean told Grace he would finish up and start bagging the trash, if she would go in and get him some water. Relieved that the work was nearly done, she jogged into the kitchen, humming to herself. She nearly tripped over the box of gardening tools in the middle of the kitchen floor.

The scream she let out was probably heard up and down the block. Sean came running, and when he saw the box, he couldn't believe his eyes. He tried to calm Grace down, telling her that they were tired and it was just a stupid mistake, etc., but she was still shaking.

By the time she got home she was much calmer and had decided not to mention it to her husband. She had started to convince herself that it was her imagination or she was over-tired, or both. The move date was next week and they had to move in. They had already signed the lease and they couldn't back out of it now.

Un-Settled In

The move went smoothly and they were all settled in their new house. It was so nice to have more room. Each of the kids had their own room now and they had lots of storage space. She had put the incident with the garden tools out of her mind completely until one night about five weeks after they'd moved in.

She was downstairs in the basement surfing the *net*. The kids were asleep in their rooms on the third floor and her husband was working on some paperwork in his new office on the second floor. Suddenly she heard footsteps running down the basement stairs. She looked up and saw her husband looking at her strangely.

"When did you come down here?" he asked.

"Um, right after you said you were going to work on those files," she replied, "Why?"

"I must be working too hard," he laughed, "I swear I heard you yelling for me. I thought you hurt yourself or something. I could have sworn you were right down the hall from me. If you screamed from down here I don't know how I could have heard you."

They brushed off this incident as a fluke until it happened again, and again, and again. It happened so often that they didn't even answer each other anymore. If someone needed help, they would have to go get the person or send one of the kids to get them. Although this was annoying, after a couple of weeks, it became routine and they barely noticed it. That didn't happen with the next thing, though.

Lights Out

Grace worked part-time about three nights a week. When she got home, she would always come in through a back door into the basement. On this night, she walked in and flipped the light switch. The basement stayed dark.

"Darn it," she thought, "the light bulb must have burned out." She felt her way along the wall to the powder room to turn that light on so she could see to change the bulb. It was out, too.

"That's weird," she thought, "I know I saw lights in the kitchen when I was pulling up."

As she began to feel her way to the basement stairs, her eyes were drawn to her computer monitor because it was on!

She could see the screen saver shimmering and the little green power light for the monitor.

Feeling that something odd was happening, she quickly went up the stairs to the kitchen and into the closet to grab some new light bulbs. Out of habit, when she opened the basement door, she flipped the switch. This time the light came on.

"No way," she thought, as she ran down the stairs to the powder room. The switch was still in the "up" or "on" position and the light was now on! She glanced over at the computer monitor. It was black now and the power light for the monitor was dark. Feeling that she might be witnessing some kind of weird electrical short circuit or something, she went to get her husband. He wasn't happy to be asked to check the electric at 10 pm when he had to work the next morning, but he did it. Grace waited in the living room, mostly afraid that there was going to be some kind of dangerous wiring that would burn the house down around them while they slept.

"Well," said her husband as he came into the living room, "I can't find anything wrong with it. Maybe you just hit the wrong switch." This started a big argument in which he accused her of over-reacting and she accused him of being insensitive. Her last shot was, "Well, you're the one who said the house was creepy!" to which he replied, "Well, you're the one who insisted we had to move here!" They went to bed angry and were still not talking to each other at breakfast.

Jake Meets a Playmate

It was pretty tense until her two sons came down. The younger one, Jake, was still at home, and Michael, the older one, went to kindergarten. Things were always hectic getting him to school, getting Jake dressed, and getting her husband off to work. This morning was more stressful than usual with the tension of the argument. The relaxing walk back from Michael's school was a very welcome relief that day. When they got home, she took Jake out back to play for a bit. He was running around the yard chasing his ball when he stopped suddenly and ran back to Grace.

"Mommy, lady stuck in tree!"

Grace looked at the tree and saw nothing.

"Mommy!" he yelled, tugging her shirt for emphasis, "Lady stuck in tree!"

The hair started to stand up on the back of her neck. "Jakey, let's go in, okay?"

She kept looking out the back window at the tree, but she didn't see anything. After they picked Michael up from school and had lunch, she sat down on the sofa for a few minutes while the boys played. Jake was laughing and it sounded like they were having fun. She had almost forgotten about the lady in the tree incident when she went out to get them a snack. Jake was laughing, but he was standing at the back window, looking out and laughing at something outside.

"Jake, "she asked, "What's so funny?"

"Lady in tree, Mommy," he answered like the answer was obvious.

Grace looked out and saw nothing. She decided she needed to say something to her husband about this. He couldn't blame this on her imagination because she wasn't seeing anything.

After an awkward exchange of apologies, he listened to her recount the exchange she witnessed with Jake and the lady. He admitted it was odd, but he also reminded her that children do have imaginary friends sometimes. He thought maybe they should look for a play group for Jake. "Maybe he just needs to be around more kids his own age," he said. Grace wished she could be so sure.

Terror in the Night

Two nights later, she woke at 3 am to Jake screaming. Both boys had bedrooms on the third floor. Jake slept in the "cold" room. "Mommy! Mommy! Mommy! Monster!" he was yelling, "Mommy! Mommy! Monster!" Thinking it was just a childhood nightmare, she asked him, "Where's the monster?"

"Monster stuck in hole!" he cried.

Grace looked around the room, but she didn't see anything. After about half an hour, she calmed him down and he went back to sleep.

The next night it was the same thing. He woke her with his screaming and she looked at the clock. It was 3 am. After five days of this, she decided to stay in his room with him to see what, if anything, was going on. She sat in a chair next to his bed, waiting and checking her watch. Right at 3:15 am, she heard what sounded like a clock ticking.

She sat in fear, just listening. She looked over at her son and saw that Jake's eyes were open and he was looking at her. Then he pointed to the window and whispered, "Mommy, monster! Mommy, monster!" She looked up to the window in dread of what she was going to see and there was a shadow. At first she thought it was the shadow from the tree, but it soon became clear it wasn't. The tree was moving back and forth on the wall as the tree outside moved with the wind, but this shadow wasn't moving. The temperature in the room started to drop and it was soon freezing in there; so cold she was shivering.

She wasn't waiting around for the next development. Grace lifted her son out of his bed and ran to the door, slamming it closed on her way out. She didn't relax until she was in the living room. Her husband came out of the bedroom and asked her what was going on. She asked him to come downstairs and stay with Jake so she could go check on Michael. She also wanted to check on Jake's room now that she felt her son was safe.

Michael was sleeping soundly and his room was nice and warm. When she looked towards Jake's room she gasped in shock. The door was wide open even though she knew she had slammed it on the way out. Cautiously, she slid over to check the room. The shadow of the tree was still there, but the other one was gone. The room was warm now, too. In spite of this, she still had an uneasy feeling, like someone was watching her. She returned to the living room and spent the night on the sofa with Jake.

In the morning, she asked Jake about the monster again and he repeated, "Monster in hole...stuck in hole." She decided to do some digging about the house.

She knew the house was over 100 years old. When she first started asking around the neighborhood, she found out that it was known as the "scary haunted house" by the neighborhood children, but no one could say how it got the reputation. The owner had died five years ago and it had been a rental house since then. The landlord had originally bought the house with plans to live there but changed his mind and decided to rent it out instead. More disturbing was that the landlord told her that the previous tenants had just abandoned the place without notice even though their rent was paid up to the next month! These things didn't prove anything on their own, but when you put them all together you have a pretty good circumstantial case for a haunting.

A Call For Help

That's when she contacted Delaware County Paranormal Research, my ghost group, to come and investigate the probable haunting in her home. We set up a date for a few days later to come and check things out, but the night before, she called it off. They had decided to just move out and she didn't want to "stir things up." She wouldn't say why she had changed her mind, but it was obvious something had really frightened her. She was now adamantly against us investigating the property and informed us that they weren't even sleeping there that night. I e-mailed her back just to check on her well-being and she said they were fine and had moved into a smaller place without any "problems." She was trying to put the house behind her.

This case represents a problem that we encounter very often as paranormal investigators. When the resident ghosts or spirits become aware that someone is going to come there to investigate, the ghosts either completely cease activity and hide or they go all out and explode in a tantrum that scares the residents so much they want nothing to do with the paranormal any more.

Bryn Mawr College

The Spirit of Higher Learning

"My one aim and concentrated purpose shall be and is to show that women can learn, can reason, can compete with men in the grand fields of literature and science ... that a woman can be a woman and a true one without having all her time engrossed by dress and society."[1]

~M. Carey Thomas

B ryn Mawr College was founded in 1885, and was the first institution of higher education to offer graduate degrees to women. M. Carey Thomas, a champion of equal educational opportunities for women, was selected as the first dean and became the second president of the college. This was her passion due to her own educational experiences. She had applied and been accepted in the doctoral program at Hopkins in Baltimore, but when they informed her that she would have to take all of her classes seated behind a screen to conceal her identity, she decided to go elsewhere. She traveled to Europe to get her doctorate, where she graduated summa cum laude.

As dean, she lived on the Bryn Mawr campus and then devoted her life to making Bryn Mawr an example of what a women's college should be—one equal to the finest research institutions in the world. She loved Bryn Mawr and was so much a part of the campus that, when she died, her ashes were placed in the cloisters of the Thomas Library. Contrary to popular belief, her body was not buried there.[1] It is also no longer a library. It is now a center for performances, meetings, and other things of that nature.

M. Carey Thomas' memorial stone in the place she loved.

Love of Learning

The Thomas Library, and especially the Gothic Cloisters, looked like something from Harry Potter's Hogwarts School of Magic. When we entered the area, we felt a sacred hushed feeling, as if we were in a church. Although there were people walking around and some construction going on outside, the noises seemed muted in the Cloisters.

I paused a moment to consider the atmosphere and there it was. Rather, there *they* were. I had heard rumors of M. Carey Thomas' ghost wandering the library and Cloisters, but I felt the

M. Carey Thomas Library doors – Is that someone welcoming us in?

Bryn Mawr College

Ghostly whispered conversations can be heard in the Cloisters.

A broken crypt-type monument has a prominent position there.

presence of at least three women. Under all the other noises, there was an undercurrent of whispering; a group of women talking back and forth as if discussing some political issue or debating a point. I concluded that this must be the spirits of these female scholars, some of whose ashes were interred here at Bryn Mawr's monument to study and knowledge, the Thomas Library, doing that which they enjoyed so much in life—discussing some academic subject at which they excelled.

In addition to M. Carey Thomas' ashes, the ground under the walkway in the Cloisters is also the final resting place for Amalie Emmy Noether, a German Jewish mathematician who fled Nazi Germany to the United States. She spent her final two years at Bryn Mawr college, from 1933 to 1935. She is described as "the most important woman in the history of mathematics."2 I have heard rumors of other burials there but cannot verify them.

Is That You, Lillian?

The first buildings on the campus were Taylor and Merion. They served as offices for general administration, classrooms, library, and a dormitory.

Merion Dorm is the location of Bryn Mawr's most famous ghost, Lillian Vickers. Versions of Lillian's story vary slightly, but they all tell of a young woman who became mentally ill, suffered some kind of breakdown, and died tragically. The most dramatic tale recounts a sudden onset of a delusion in which Lillian believed she had somehow contracted leprosy. In a state of desperation, she doused herself with some type of flammable liquid. Some storytellers claim she set herself on fire accidentally, others claim it was intentional suicide. Either way, she ended up dying in terrible agony.

This story, farfetched as it sounds, was often dismissed as legend until *The Bi-College News* published an article about Lillian on February 1, 2000. The author of the article references a letter from the Bryn Mawr archives from someone at the college to Lillian's father in California. The letter says "the Bryn Mawr community had been concerned about Lillian's mental state for…two weeks prior to her death."3

This was 1903. At that time, most women did not go to college, especially across the country from their home. If Lillian did this, she must have been a very intelligent, independent woman who truly valued learning. She was described as "witty and popular."[3] That makes what happened so tragic. It is not known what caused this rapid decline in her mental state. Perhaps she was stressed or worried about something else. She may have had a personal problem that became overwhelming for her. Whatever it was, it caused Lillian's dream of higher education to literally go up in flames.

Lillian had developed the delusion that she had leprosy. "Those who knew her traced this belief back to her encounter with a fundamentalist missionary from the Christian Union, who had diagnosed her with this disease."[3] The author of the letter acknowledged that Lillian had seen a doctor and that the doctor had been optimistic about Lillian's recovery. Unfortunately, little was known about mental illness then. Lillian was able to lock herself in a bathroom. Her friends, who had been watching her, tried to force the door open. When the door opened, they saw to their horror that their friend had somehow set herself on fire. She was taken to a hospital where she died a few hours later.

"The letter's writer says that when she visited Lillian in the hospital, [Lillian] asked me to forgive her for the harm her death had done to the College ... I did everything I could to console her and tell her she was not responsible, but throughout our conversation she assumed that she had killed herself in order to avoid being dangerous to other people ..."[3]

Does this remorse cause Lillian to still stalk the halls of Merion? Her glowing ghost has been seen on the third floor of the dormitory and she is said to open and close doors and cause problems with electronic equipment. As we passed this dorm during my first visit, there was a distinct feeling of someone watching us from these windows. I took a walk over to the door to see which building it was. It was Merion Hall.

We weren't allowed inside this dorm building. When I got home, I looked to see what I could find out from the website. From

Is Lillian Vickers still lurking at Merion Hall?

the floor plans on www.brynmawr.edu, the watcher appeared to be on the third floor, and appeared to be in a bathroom! Was it Lillian Vickers? I sent her out a little "hello" in case it was.

The Showering Spirit

Rhoads Hall, across the campus from Merion, is the home of a playful ghost who apparently likes her privacy and still enjoys taking a shower! I came across this story in an article called "Ghost Stories: Popular Tales about the Lost Souls of Bryn Mawr" that appeared in the December 8, 2004 issue of *The College News*. The article listed several places that were reported to be haunted on campus. Most of the accounts seemed like the typical stories that make the rounds of colleges and universities all over campus, but the one at Rhoads Hall struck me as such an odd account that it is likely to be true.

The ghost at Rhoads Hall was first reported by a public safety officer whose job involved walking rounds through the empty dorms to make sure no one was there and nothing was amiss. As he was walking down a third floor hallway, the uneventful silence that had marked his rounds were interrupted by a loud scraping noise in one of the rooms. He walked over to the door and jiggled the handle. It was locked. He knocked loudly on the door and said, "Public Safety! This building is off limits! Open the door now." He was answered with more of the same scraping noise. Unsure of what or who was inside, he went to get another officer for backup and they entered the room. There was no one there and nothing looked out of place. He left the room, locked the door, and walked down the hallway shaking his head. Sometimes walking through old empty buildings can get to you, so the incident was laughed off until the next one happened.

On another shift, the same officer, walking through the third floor of Rhoads Hall, heard a shower running in the third-floor bathroom. He stepped up to the door and announced, "Public Safety!" The water stopped, but no one came out. He then walked through the bathroom, checking each stall. They were all empty. (It is not known whether one of them was wet or not.)

When he told his fellow officers about the shower, they were laughing *at* him this time instead of *with* him, as they had over the noisy dorm room. To humor the now nervous officer, the supervisor agreed to do the rounds of Rhoads Hall the next shift. When the officers returned at the end of that shift, the supervisor had a funny look on his face and announced that rounds would no longer include walking inside Rhoads Hall. They would now just check it by walking around the outside of the building. What happened to cause him to make this decision is not known.

The reason I include this story is because the incidents are so typical of what is reported at a haunted location that it is likely that this story is true. While there could have been any number of explanations for the scraping sound in the dorm room, there is no way someone could have gotten out of the bathroom without being seen by the safety officer. Most hauntings are marked by subtle incidents like misplaced items, unexplained noises, opening doors, and running water—incidents that could just as easily be caused by a human agent. The incidents are often widely spaced, as well, so that the witness begins to doubt his or her own perception of the event until something else happens. At some point, the incidents become too numerous to be dismissed as chance or mistaken identity and then the scale tips in favor of their being an unseen entity on the scene.

While I felt nothing out of the ordinary when I stood outside Rhoads Hall, I wasn't inside, alone, at a time when the campus was quiet.

That Feeling of Being Followed...

As we walked back towards the admissions office, we passed by Taylor Hall. When we initially passed by on the way to other buildings, I had felt like someone was watching us from that building. I felt like that same someone was following us as we passed by Taylor Hall on the way out, so much so that I missed everything the guide was telling us about it. We went in and, as she was talking, I felt a presence watching us from the hallway. I took one photo and then paused for a moment. I said to the spirit, "I can tell you are here and you are with us. I would like to see you. If you will allow me to take your picture, I would be grateful." (The photo was not large enough to use here, but you can see it at: www.delcoghosts.com.)

I couldn't get a name or a picture of who it was exactly, just that it was female. I could feel her presence continue to follow us as we made our way back to the admissions office. We chatted with the admissions staff for a bit and then went on our way, discussing the next location we wanted to visit. Perhaps we should have been paying more attention to whether someone was still with us or not because things got really interesting on the drive home.

As we traveled south on the Blue Route, my daughter and I both kept seeing someone out of the corner of our eyes by the sides of the road. As we came down the ramp for our exit, the talk show we had been listening to on the radio show cut out and an announcer came on, naming the song that was coming up next. We didn't recognize it and the announcer's voice sounded like one of those old radio shows from the 1930s. The song began. It was a woman singing a song I didn't recognize but it also sounded like a song from the 1930s or 40s. I looked at the radio and there was now no number showing where the station normally displays. I hit the number two button, which was the button for the talk station we had been listening to and the talk show came back on. Remarking how odd that was, I started hitting other buttons, looking for the strange station that had broken in. I could not find it. I hit the seek button. There was nothing that sounded remotely like it. I wish now that I had just left the station on.

What was it? I tend to think that it may have something to do with the fact that I had recently begun experimenting with the ghost box, which uses a scan of the am dial to help reveal voices from the other side. Was it a spirit from Bryn Mawr College trying to communicate with us through the AM radio? I visited at least one location a week for about twelve weeks during that time and that was the only time radio incident ever happened, so I like to think so. I am just sorry I didn't realize it at the time and I missed her message.

The Visitor in the Hallway at Taylor Hall.

Gladwyne Ghosts

A Gladwyne Ghost Story

Brad enjoys treasure hunting. His treasures are old coins, buttons, and other artifacts that he finds with his metal detector. Display cases of all sizes decorate his home in Gladwyne, each with a display of some of the buried treasures he has discovered. He invited us to investigate his home and find out a little more about who the ghosts were and what they wanted. Hopefully, he would see something that night. Although several people had seen and heard the ghosts in and around Brad's home, he had never seen or heard anything himself.

The first room that I paused in was the dining room. It had an odd, unsettled feeling to it. I asked someone to take some photos, and in the area where I felt the largest concentration of energy, there were orb anomalies. We went through the room to check the levels of electromagnetic energy, but nothing unusual registered.

Brad wasn't surprised by what we felt in the dining room. That room was the first one where anyone experienced anything. The day they moved in, his mother was over at the house helping unpack. She was alone in the dining room when she heard a man's voice behind her. "Help Me!" it urged. "Help me." She turned around quickly to find the same pile of boxes that had been there all along. Shrugging it off, she went back to work. She had just put the voice out if her mind when there it was again, "Help me!" With that, she decided to wait outside until Brad returned with the next load of boxes.

When he arrived, she told him what had happened. He checked around for a radio, an open window, or anything that could have been a source for the voice. He found nothing, but he remembered what the people he'd had bought the house from told him.

The dining room had been the bedroom for the old man who lived there. They had it set up as a hospital room so he could be cared for after he had been diagnosed with an aggressive form of cancer. The man had died in that room and then his heirs sold the house to Brad. He wasn't sure if this was something he should tell his mother, though. She seemed upset and he really needed help unpacking and cleaning up.

A couple of days later she was back at the house, cleaning and organizing things for him. Brad left to get some lunch for them. When he came back, she was gone. He found her cigarette burning in the ashtray, so she must have left in a big hurry. When he called her to ask what had happened, she refused to talk about it. Despite repeated questioning, she has never told him what happened that day, nor has she ever permitted herself to be alone in his house.

We moved then to the second floor, where I received a strong image of a soldier. I wasn't sure what type of soldier he was, but as I described his clothing, I saw Brad begin nodding. "He has been seen all over the property, not just in the house," Brad offered. Our group history expert said that my description marked him as a Pennsylvania militia or "minuteman" from the American Revolution. Brad then said that, in addition to the soldier being seen in various areas of the house, including the basement, he had also been spotted by Brad's neighbor. The neighbor saw what he thought was a Revolutionary War soldier standing in the back yard one night. He said he looked a lot like the typical drawings you see of Revolutionary War Patriots. As soon as he saw him, the soldier vanished.

The soldier had next appeared in Brad's garage one night. A friend was visiting and parked his car in the garage. As he stepped out of the car and turned, he saw the soldier, which he described as a "Revolutionary War-looking soldier" who vanished as soon as he saw him. Since he has been seen in so many places, we think that it is more likely that this ghost is connected with the property and not the house.

Not much is known about the history of the property before the house was built. The area that is now Gladwyne was settled in 1682 by Welsh Quakers and was originally called Merion Square. In 1891, the whole Main Line became fashionable when wealthy people from Philadelphia began building summer homes there. Merion Square was renamed "Gladwyne" in imitation of some of the neighboring Welsh-sounding towns like Bala Cynwyd and Bryn Mawr. Unlike those names, Gladwyne is a fanciful word; it has no meaning in Welsh. The British and Patriots passed through the area often on their way from Brandywine to Philadelphia and then to Valley Forge. During the whole Philadelphia campaign, from the late summer of 1777 into the following year, the troops often foraged in the countryside for supplies, so they really were all over the entire area.

The last area we explored in the house was the attic. Immediately, we were aware of a female presence, but I didn't see anything. Our other team psychic, Faith, immediately began describing a woman in a Victorian dress with dark hair who was searching for some item she had lost. Faith was so certain that there was something hidden there that she got down on her hands and knees and crawled through one of the storage areas.

Brad was obviously dying to tell us something. First, he assured us and Faith that there was no way there was anything hidden in the house. Since his hobby was finding small hidden treasures, he had already gone over the entire house and property. Then he told us about the incident that really convinced him the house was haunted and caused him to get a more professional opinion on it.

He had allowed a couple that he was friends with to stay in the attic temporarily. One morning, the woman had an interesting story to tell. She had awakened in the night

What was hidden in the crawlspace?

because she felt something pressing down on her, as if it were trying to wake her. She tried to turn over to escape the pressure and felt what she was sure was a hand slapping her in the face. At that, she woke up completely, but whatever it was had vanished. This presence in the attic had been undetected until now—but no one had been sleeping in the attic until now. He had half-dismissed this as a bad dream until another female friend was going towards the attic stairs and saw a woman in a Victorian-style dress sitting on the stairs. She told Brad that the woman had appeared to be completely solid and she wasn't sure what she was seeing until the woman suddenly disappeared.

Although we didn't see her that night or when we returned again to try and communicate with her, we were all positive she was there. I remembered that Brad said that the ghosts had never shown themselves to him and he was with us the entire night. It was possible that the ghosts were "hiding" from him.

When he'd gotten married, he must have decided that there could only be one "lady of the house" and he called a friend of his who was also an Episcopal priest to come and bless the home. Since then, no one has seen her, but experience has taught me that these "blessings" often wear off. I prefer the answer I received one day from my guide during meditation. "When the lady finds what she is searching for, she will be finished here." Maybe she was looking for the right "lady of the house" to take over for her, and now that Brad has found her, the Victorian lady has moved on.

The Phantom Horseman of Old Gulph Road

Around the late nineteenth century, the tale of a phantom horseman began to make the rounds of Gladwyne. There was a deserted house on Old Gulph Road that had been the scene of a duel a century before. Every night since, the ghost of a Revolutionary War cavalryman was seen galloping around the house; sword ablaze.

The story went that the soldier had learned of his love interest's tryst with another man and challenged the man to a duel. I suppose the winner got the cheating girlfriend. Not much of a prize, in my opinion, but why ruin a good story with logic?

The heartbroken suitor was killed in the duel and now spends eternity re-enacting his frantic ride around his sweetheart's house.

Haverford State Hospital

The big abandoned mental hospital that was an attraction for teenagers, urban explorers, and ghost hunters is no longer standing. In 1998, the state of Pennsylvania closed the "Haverford Hilton" because it had become obsolete. Methods for treating mental illness had changed significantly since it was opened in 1964. Better medications are available and there is greater public awareness of the nature of mental illness. Legally, individuals with disabilities now have the right to be in the least restrictive environment possible for them, and for most of these people, an inpatient program is just too restrictive.

During Joanne Silberner's journalistic investigation of the hospital and its closing, she interviewed former employees that claimed "conditions declined in the 1970s. Overcrowding meant patients might sleep in hallways or dayrooms. Many were kept in seclusion and restraints, heavily drugged, or subjected to shock treatments as a form of discipline."[1] By the time conditions at the hospital were improved in the 1990s, new treatment methods and legislation had made outpatient treatment more routine and Haverford State became a dinosaur. Now, the institution's buildings have been demolished and the land they once occupied are going to be transformed into a complex that includes bike and walking trails, ball fields, an amphitheater, and a picnic area. There are also plans for retirement communities and other small housing developments.

Paranormal Investigation groups that requested permission to enter the abandoned hospital complex to investigate it before the demolition were denied. However, despite the threats of arrest and fines for trespassing, teenagers and urban explorers regularly visited the site before and during its demolition. Many of these people reported strange experiences. I would

Haverford State's entrance. *Courtesy of Lori Clarke of Clark Photography*

put this down to overactive imagination in a dark, abandoned mental hospital, but they all independently report the same experiences in the same places. These were not second hand, but firsthand accounts from the people who had actually been there.

One young lady swore there was some kind of presence in what she described as the former surgical procedures room. She had an overwhelming feeling that something in there wanted her to leave. When she finally convinced her friends to go, they heard the door slam shut behind them as they exited. Another young woman who had explored the abandoned building said that when she entered a room that appeared to be some kind of surgical unit, she was overwhelmed by images and feelings of people being tortured there.

Others I spoke to felt that there was what they described as a dark, evil presence in the morgue. Two of the people I spoke

Hallway leading to the morgue and home of a dark presence.
Courtesy of Lori Clarke of Clark Photography

to about their experiences there were so unnerved in that area of the former hospital they couldn't even enter the morgue, but turned back and ran down the hallway without going in.

One woman's father was a patient in Haverford State Hospital in 1973 as part of a detox program. This was during the time when conditions were declining there. She asked him if it was haunted or if anything weird had happened while he was there. She had visited the former hospital on the community open house day held prior to demolition and had experienced a negative presence near the morgue. He told her that during his stay there, another patient in the program with him overdosed and died. After that, they kept hearing bangs on the wall where his bed was, but when they looked for the source of the noise, they couldn't find anything. Her father stated that they all felt it was the spirit of the man who had overdosed, desperately banging on the wall for help.

A few guys went there about three years before the demolition to nose around in the old buildings. They heard there was a morgue there and that was high on their list of places to see. They did locate the morgue and had a look around. Suddenly, the metal doors flew open and then slammed shut. They all froze, thinking either someone else was in there, trying to scare them, or they had just been caught trespassing. The doors flew open and slammed shut again. They concluded that it must be another explorer playing around because security would have said something by now. Hoping to surprise the jokesters, a couple of them sneaked out while the others kept talking in the morgue, so the jokers would think they were all still in there. The two guys who snuck out to the doors reached them to find that there was no one there. They went back to the morgue, thinking they had just missed whoever it was, when they heard the doors fly open and slam shut again. This time they all ran out to confront the person, but the place was empty. They didn't hear any retreating footsteps, and after a quick look around the area, it was clear that they were alone. Who was opening and

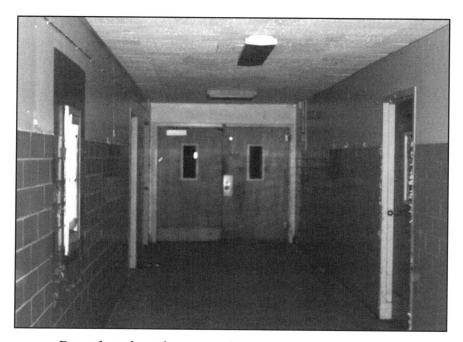

Doors have been known to slam open and closed by themselves.
Courtesy of Lori Clarke of Clark Photography

slamming the doors? They didn't stick around long enough for it to happen again.

About a year after the door slamming incident, two friends ventured in to the derelict building with hopes of seeing the morgue. As they were walking down the hallway, one of the men heard a growling breath by his ear. Assuming it was his companion trying scare him, he said, "Stop that!" in a stern stage whisper. His friend stopped walking and asked, "Stop what? What are you talking about?"

"It's not funny and I'm not scared, so just quit it," said the first guy. His friend seemed genuinely confused. "I didn't do anything!" he declared. The man who heard the growling just shook his head and started walking again. They were almost at the morgue when he heard the growling breath by his ear again. This time he turned to his buddy and yelled, "Stop that!"

"What are you talking about?" asked his friend.

"I heard a growling breathy noise right by my ear. I know it was you, messing with me, so just stop," he explained. He really wanted to see the morgue and maybe some of the other spots he'd heard about and he didn't feel like having to listen to his friend making spooky noises the whole time. It was obvious he was losing patience, so he was a little unnerved when his friend still insisted that he was not making the noise. Just to be sure, he told his friend to walk behind him instead of next to him.

A few seconds later, with his friend walking behind him, they could see the doorway to the morgue. Without any warning the growling returned, only this time it was right in his face and much louder than before. Aware that his friend was behind him, he stopped and peered into the darkness in front of him.

"Did you hear something again?" his friend asked nervously. He didn't answer him, but began backing slowly towards him, now certain there was something threatening in the darkness ahead. When he reached his buddy's side, he gripped his arm and whispered, "Let's get out of here now!"

"We didn't get to see anything," his friend uttered.

"There is something in here with us...something that doesn't want us here," he explained, pulling his companion backwards with him, towards the exit. When they reached the end of the hallway, they turned and ran. They never made it to the morgue. On reflection, he doesn't regret having not seen it. He doesn't know what was in there that day, only that it wasn't a living person.

Was it a warning of impending danger? Was it the same menacing presence felt by others who also approached the morgue and found themselves unable to enter?

Those two friends weren't the last to run into the morgue's threatening guardian. During the Township's open house of the grounds, a local woman visited with her husband and family. They entered through the building that had once housed the juvenile treatment center. She reported feeling an intense anxious expectation, as if someone were about to leap from one of the rooms. The aura of anxiety and sadness increased and became so oppressive that she nearly panicked and left. She headed towards the door at the end of the hallway and found it was chained shut. They had to backtrack through the building. As soon as she got outside, she felt a huge sense of relief.

The morgue was one of the things she wanted to see and photograph. With a general idea of where it was located, she headed towards it with her husband. They located the hallway leading to the morgue and started down it. She was almost at the morgue when she stopped. The area was so saturated with what she described as feelings of dread and evil, that she turned and went back outside. Her husband followed.

Disappointed that she didn't get the photos she wanted, she decided to make another attempt at reaching the morgue. Fortified with a few gulps of fresh air and some sunshine, she headed back inside and walked towards the morgue. Once again, she was overwhelmed by that feeling of dread. She was sure there was something evil down the hall, waiting for her to come in. She feels that if she had gone any further, that she may never have come back.

After a moment of hesitation, where she tried to overcome the threatening presence with the excitement of the photos she would get, the spirit of caution won and she turned and left. To her dismay, she heard footsteps behind her. Hoping the footsteps were attached to a person, she turned to face them. The hallway was empty, but the footsteps continued to advance towards her. She stood her ground as they passed right by. A giggle echoed down the hallway from the direction the footsteps took. She'd had enough. She got out of there as quickly as she could and never returned.

As I heard these experiences, I couldn't help but think that there were never so many people trying desperately to get into a morgue. If these accounts had taken place in the morgue, I would probably attribute them to just jumpiness that one would expect to feel in a place like a morgue or a funeral home. These things happened in the hallway, though, and each person reported a feeling of dread and evil. Was it a residual energy left over from some unknown evil act committed there? The interactive aspects of the growling and the footsteps point to an intelligent entity.

The buildings are now demolished. Have the spirits been carried away with the refuse? Are they dormant, waiting for new life and energy to occupy the space and reactivate the haunting presences there? One source theorized that the reason no paranormal groups were allowed to investigate was because there was something evil there and the *powers that be* didn't want that presence verified. If these witnesses are accurate in their descriptions of what they experienced there, I can't help but wonder which part of the new construction will be where the morgue used to be.

A ghostly presence in the hallway at Haverford State.
Courtesy of Lori Clarke of Clark Photography

Detail of previous photo. *Courtesy of Lori Clarke of Clark Photography*

So what happened to these ghosts? Since no one was ever allowed in the hospital to investigate formally and try to help the spirits move on, they are probably still there!

All of the photos of Haverford State were taken and courteously made available for this publication by Lori Clarke of Clark Photography, http://drummie.smugmug.com/.

Philly's Main Line Haunts

I n my research into the ghosts of Lower Merion and Main Line areas, I found that there really were ghosts everywhere. Passing through the area on Montgomery Avenue, you'll see a historic building or home right next door to a brand new shop or home. This is an area where the past really mixes with the present in a way that is visible in its landscape and invisible in its many ghosts and legends. Long-time residents often know of a few haunted places and newcomers are often pleasantly surprised at the number of ghosts and legends that abound in the area. Take some time to stop and visit some of the places in this area that is so full of history and haunted places.

Bibliography

Introduction:
1. http://www.lenapelifeways.org/lenape3.htm
2. http://www.lowermerionhistory.org/texts/first300/part02.html

The General Wayne Inn
1. http://www.ushistory.org/tour/tour_poe.htm
O'Reilly, David. "A Ghost Story." *Philadelphia Inquirer*, October 29, 1992

The Wayne Family
1. Stille, Charles J., *Major-General Anthony Wayne and the Pennsylvania Line in the Continental Army*, Philadelphia, J.B. Lippincott Co., 1893, p 343.
2. _____. *History of Erie County, Pennsylvania*, vol. 1, Chicago, Warner, Beers & Co, 1884, pp. 211 - 212.
Norman, Michael and Beth Scott. *Historic Haunted America*. Tor Books. 2006
Norman, Michael and Beth Scott. *Haunted Heartland*. Marlboro Books. 1991.
Norman, Michael and Beth Scott. *Haunted Heritage*. Tor Books. 2002

Paoli Battlefield
1. Tucker, Glenn. *Mad Anthony Wayne and the New Nation*, Harrisburg: Stackpole Books, 1973.
http://www.ushistory.org/paoli/info/faq.htm
Tredyffrin Easttown History Club Quarterly, January, 2003, Vol., XVI, No. 1.

Harriton House
Baker, Ronald L. *Hoosier Folk Legends*. Indiana University Press, 1984.
http://www.harriton.org
http://www.archives.upenn.edu/histy/features/1700s/people/thomson_chas.html

John Roberts House
1. http://www.lowermerionhistory.org/texts/first300/part07.html
Ilgenfritz, Richard. "Ghosts of the Main Line". *Main Line Times*, 10/30/03.

The Blue Ball Inn
1. *Tredyffrin Easttown History Club Quarterly* – History Nook
http://www.tredyffrin.org/pdf/newsletters/1998-fall-newsletter.pdf

The Clockmaker's Ghost
Uncle Ben, "Legends of Penn Valley: Dark Crime and Spooks", *Main Line Chronicle*, May 24, 1962.

Rathalla of Rosemont
1. *First 300: The Amazing and Rich History of Lower Merion* by LMHS, American Society of Civil Engineers; Limited edition, March 2000.
Kelly, Sister Maria Stella, and Brenda Reigle. Joseph Sinnott Mansion [Rosemont College]. National Register of Historic Places designation report. Washington, D.C.: U.S. Department of the Interior/ National Park Service, 1980.
Main Building, Rosemont College. Booklet. Second ed.. Rosemont, PA: Rosemount College, 2003.

Cabrini College Ghosts
Loquitor Issues: 10/30/03—"The Haunted" by Angelina Wagner and "Cabrini Ghosts: Fact or Fiction" by Jessica Marella 10/28/04; "Cabrini's Mansion: Ghost Stories still float around campus" by Domenique Pinho, 10/28/05; "Welcome to the Haunted Mansion" by Elizabeth Brachelli, 8/31/06. Available online at http://www.loquitor.com.
Morrison, William. *The Main Line Country Houses*, 1870-1930. New York: Acanthus Press, 2002.

A Deadly Love Triangle
King, Moses. King's Views of Philadelphia. Illustrated Monographs. Part 6. Moses King, New York, 1900.
Muldoon, Sylvan. *Psychic Experiences of Famous People*, Kessinger Publishing, LLC, 2007.

Westminster Cemetery
1. Brunvand, Jan Harold. *The Vanishing Hitchhiker: American Urban Legends & Their Meanings.* New York: W.W. Norton & Company, Inc., 1981
Main Line Chronicle, "Lower Merion's Spooks, Haunted Houses and Ghostly Legends". October 27, 2976.

Bryn Mawr College
1. Helen Lefkowitz Horowitz, *The Power and Passion of M. Carey Thomas*, New York: Knopf, 1994.
2. Dick, Auguste. Emmy Noether: 1882-1935. 1980
3. Friedman, Leeza. "Legend of Merion Ghost continues to haunt Bryn Mawr." *Bi-College News*, February 1, 2000.

Haverford State Hospital
1. Silberner, Joanne. "The Closing of Haverford State." *The Infinite Mind*, June 21, 2000. http://www.lcmedia.com/mindprgm.htm
Photos from Lori Clarke; http://drummie.smugmug.com/

Index